Preaching Through the Bible

1 Kings

Michael Eaton

Sovereign World

Sovereign World
PO Box 777
Tonbridge
Kent TN11 9XT
England

By the same author:

Ecclesiastes (Tyndale Commentary) – IVP
The Baptism with the Spirit – IVP
How to Live a Godly Life – Sovereign World
Walk in the Spirit – Word
Living Under Grace (Romans 6–7) – Nelson Word
Preaching Through the Bible (1 Samuel) – Sovereign World
Preaching Through the Bible (2 Samuel) – Sovereign World

ISBN: 1 85240 176 7

Typeset by CRB Associates, Norwich
Printed in England by Clays Ltd, St Ives plc

Preface

There is need of a series of biblical expositions which are especially appropriate for English-speaking preachers in the Third World. Such expositions need to be laid out in such a way that they will be useful to those who put their material to others in clear points. They need to avoid difficult vocabulary and advanced grammatical structures. They need to avoid European or North American illustrations. *Preaching Through the Bible* seeks to meet such a need. Although intended for an international audience I have no doubt that their simplicity will be of interest to many first-language speakers of English as well.

These expositions will take into account the Hebrew and Greek texts but will also take into account three translations of the Bible, the New King James (or Revised Authorised) Version, the New American Standard Version and the New International Version. The expositions will be comprehensible whichever of these versions is used, and no doubt with some others as well. At times the expositor will simply translate the Hebrew or Greek himself.

It is not our purpose to deal with minute exegetical detail, although the commentator often has to do work of this nature as part of his preliminary preparation. But just as a good housewife likes to serve a good meal rather than display her pots and pans, so the good expositor is concerned with the 'good meal' of Scripture rather than the 'pots and pans' of dictionaries, disputed interpretations and the like. Only occasionally will such matters have to be discussed. Similarly matters of 'Introduction' do not receive detailed discussion. A simple outline of some 'introductory' matters is to be found in the appendix to the exposition but the first chapter gets immediately into the message of Scripture.

Michael A. Eaton
Nairobi

Contents

Contents

Author's Preface

This is the third of my expositions of the books of Samuel and Kings, and follows the pattern of my *1 Samuel* and *2 Samuel*.

I am grateful for the support of family and friends who encourage my preaching and writing. Friends in Nairobi City Hall lunchtime meetings, in the Discipleship School, in Central Church, in KICC Chrisco Church, and other Chrisco venues, heard these chapters before anyone else. They are precious friends indeed.

A further opportunity was given me to preach through 1 Kings when I travelled to Western Kenya at the end of 1994 with friends from Nairobi. To Pastor Abiud Kimathi of Kisumu, and his wife Mary, to Stephen Onyango who arranged my stay in Alupe, I owe my thanks. The expositions of 1 Kings 16–22 were preached also in Kakamega over the Christmas holiday, 1994, where I travelled with friends from Kawangware Restoration Centre, Nairobi. I am grateful to Pastor Evans Mukhwana, and his wife Mary, in whose up-country home I stayed at that time, and to Mrs Florence Okumu who contributed to these pages and, *'drawing a bow at a venture'* (1 Kings 22:34), shared in the preaching of them in Kakamega. Asante sana!

To Jenny; to Tina Gysling, my daughter, who works through my material; to my son Calvin who is an ever-present help in time of computer-trouble; to Chris Mungeam, a faithful friend – many thanks. One of them asked 'Why does the word "may" come so often in chapter 17?' I answered 'Because often God does not reward us according to our iniquities'.

Michael A. Eaton

Chapter 1

God Protects His King

(1 Kings 1:1–27)

The books of 1 and 2 Kings deal with kingship (as their names suggest). Kingship or kingdom is an important theme in the Bible, and 1–2 Kings will help us understand it. 'Kings' is the story of how God was looking for a perfect king. David was God's king, the man after God's own heart. Could there be another king like David? Not until Jesus! Only **Jesus** is the perfect Son of David! The main point of the book is that the kings of Israel failed because of idolatry; idolatry is fatal! 'Kings' presses home the teaching of Deuteronomy, with its warnings against false gods.

So God's salvation is called 'God kingdom' and we are to seek first His kingdom (Matthew 6:33). We should all be interested in kingship. We reign with Christ. Jesus is a King, and we are kings under Him, sharing His throne.

At the time when our story begins, David is suffering from the problems of old age (1 Kings 1:1), and his servants find an attractive young woman to keep him warm (1:2–4). The kingdom of God is in danger, for Adonijah is eager to steal the kingdom.

The question is: how will God's kingdom continue? Something is happening to David that will never happen to Jesus, God's ultimate king. David's kingship is obviously coming to an end. He has been truly a God-appointed king, and had been greatly used by God, but Adonijah is not the Lord's anointed.

1. **Solomon is being called to rise up to kingship** (1 Kings 1:1–4). Solomon will soon be called to be the king, first alongside David and then succeeding David. All Christians are called to rise up to kingship, to rule for God, to a sense of direction, to liberty, to victory and triumph. This is not arrogance or pride, but a true sense of reigning with Jesus Christ.

2. **Solomon has to learn to rise to kingship despite opposition** (1 Kings 1:5–10). Adonijah is an enemy who wants dominion. We too will find many obstacles that rise up against God's will that we should reign and rule in Christ. In our own tendencies to sin, in a thousand adverse circumstances, in the attacks of Satan, we shall find many forces standing against us. Adonijah said 'I will oppose Solomon; I will be king instead'. Solomon had to face enmity, but in the end Solomon won! He did become the king. The gates of hell do not prevail over God's king or God's kingdom.

3. **There is a right way and a wrong way of being ambitious in God's kingdom**. God wants us to reign in Christ, but it is a mistake to seek kingship the way Adonijah did. He wanted to be king but without heeding the will of God. God had chosen Solomon; Adonijah's ambition was against God's will for his life. It was sheer worldliness. Adonijah was not called and anointed as Saul and David were. Both of the two previous kings had been given kingship by God.

Ambition is not wrong in itself. James and John were ambitious (Matthew 20:20–23), yet Jesus never rebuked them for their desire to serve Him in His kingdom. But ambition needs to be refined and purified. God will give us the desires of our hearts, but it has to be in His time, in His way, and our desires have to line up with His desires for us.

We do not choose ourselves. God has got a will for our lives. He will reveal that will to us. There is no need to manipulate. Ambition damages the progress of the kingship.

Adonijah was self-appointed (1 Kings 1:5, he *'exalted himself...'*). He was acting a part. He was acting as though he were king, seeking to present a certain kind of 'image' for himself (1 Kings 1:5b). His ambition came from self-will and pride (1 Kings 1:6). He had never been rebuked and was constantly admired. He gets the civic and the religious leaders on his side in a conspiracy (1 Kings 1:7). Adonijah was David's son, and Joab was David's nephew, the son of his sister. Adonijah was dividing a family that should have been working together. Also in the conspiracy was Abiathar, who also was an ambitious man, in rivalry with Zadok. How often the kingdom of God comes under attack by the rivalry of its participants. Adonijah was acting without any unanimity or spiritual submission (1 Kings 1:8). He was divisive (1 Kings 1:9–10). He was a trickster. He arranges a great religious festival in which he wants to get himself proclaimed king.

What then was the right way of being ambitious? Solomon was apparently doing nothing! He was just trusting God to act on his behalf. If God had truly chosen him as the next king, God would bring it about.

4. **The kingdom was saved by boldness and faith**. Solomon got his kingdom because others were willing to take action for him. It needed God's people to be willing to act. Adonijah would have got away with his trick if God's people had simply done nothing. Solomon was right to do nothing, but Nathan and Bathsheba were right to take action! It took great courage to do what Nathan did. If he had failed he would undoubtedly have lost his life. Yet he was decisive. When he had seen what needed to be done he did it boldly. He was wise to go through Bathsheba. David was more likely to listen to Bathsheba. She was closer to him than Nathan was (1 Kings 1:11). He was practical and had something practical to suggest to Bathsheba (1 Kings 1:12). He knows the right way to get David to take notice of what is happening. He is persuasive (1:12) and he helps her to persuade David (1:13). He is wise in arranging for a double witness (1 Kings 1:14). By going separately it was clear that Bathsheba was not just indulging in gossip or ambition. It would make it clear that the matter was serious.

Bathsheba shows no resentment against Abishag (1:15). David is her husband, and he is old, but he is God's king. So

11

she shows him a lot of respect (1:16). She puts the facts before David (1 Kings 1:17–21). She is also persuasive and does not blame him or criticize him. She quotes his promise. David is a man who will keep his word (1:17). She underlines the seriousness of the situation (1:18–19) and reminds him of his responsibility (1:20). She appeals to his love for her and for Solomon (1:21). She has become a spiritual woman.

Then Nathan comes in again and presents a similar appeal (1 Kings 1:22–27). Between Nathan and Bathsheba, the kingdom is saved. If we are alert to the needs of the hour and ready to act decisively and wisely when God calls upon us to act, we shall be used by God to protect His kingdom.

Chapter 2

How God's Kingdom Works
(1 Kings 1:28–53)

In the story of how Solomon reached the throne we have a picture of how kingship works in practise. We are seeing the way in which God rules. It is good to see it, for Jesus is our king and we reign with Him.

1. **The kingdom of God brings revival** (1:28–32). Consider David. He truly is God's king. He was chosen by God and put in office by God. The true king is always put in office by God; he is never a pretender like Adonijah.

But at the point where we are seeing him, David is weary and exhausted with age. He has been suffering from slow circulation of the blood (1:1). His rebellious son is doing what he likes, feeling that David is too old and weak to do anything about it.

But God's kings can be revived. Suddenly David is alert. 'Call Bathsheba!' (1:28). 'Call Zadok! Get Nathan! Bring Benaiah!' (1:32). Apparently from out of nowhere David gets his old energy and drive back again. He takes command. He acts authoritatively. He summons a prophet (Nathan), a priest (Zadok), a soldier (Benaiah). He knows what to do. The oath that he had sworn to Solomon that Solomon would be king must be publicly renewed and Solomon must become joint-king with David immediately. If Adonijah has planned a coup, David has the drive and energy to speedily appoint Solomon as king jointly with David in a way that no one will dare resist.

Where did David get this sudden energy and drive and skill from? God's kings get revived! David himself had written in one of his psalms *'Though I walk in the midst of trouble, you will revive me'* (Psalm 138:7; see also Psalm 119:154b). Now he was experiencing the truth of what he had said.

2. **The kingdom of God brings anointing** (1:33–37). At one point Solomon was weak and seemed to be powerless. He was appointed as king but there did not seem to be much chance of this coming to pass. Suddenly David, the greater king, acts and appoints a junior king. This is what Jesus wants to do for us. The Lord is a *'great king'*, says Psalm 47:2 (see also Psalm 95:3; Malachi 1:14). As David the great king appointed one to be a junior king with him and under him, so our King, our Jesus, does the same for us. He is the supreme King, but we reign under Him.

Solomon got anointed. Oil was poured over him to symbolise that he would be given enabling power to be God's king. We too get the anointing of God's oil, God's Holy Spirit. Three types of support came to Solomon. He had the support of prophecy, the work of Nathan the prophet. He had the support of intercession, the work of Zadok the priest. He had the support of powerful protection, the work of Benaiah the soldier.

The Christian reigns with Christ. He is given the anointing of the Spirit. He is to be in abundant fellowship and support, in a church where there is (i) prophetic ministry, powerful speaking from God, where there is (ii) priestly ministry, powerful intercession, and where there is (iii) an army for God and mighty warriors for God. The Christian reigns with Christ in the midst of prophecy, priesthood and power.

3. **The kingdom of God brings opposition** (1:38–49). Solomon had suporting him a prophet, a priest and a true soldier. He had against him a self-appointed king, a backslidden priest, and a traitor with killer instincts. Adonijah was a self-appointed king and had no true interest in reigning for God. He was reigning in the interests of

self-promotion. Adonijah got the support of Joab a defector from David's cause, a man of violence, who had murdered Abner out of revenge (2 Samuel 2:23; 3:27, 30), and had killed Uriah (2 Samuel 11:6–26) and Absalom (2 Samuel 18:14–33) and Amasa (2 Samuel 20:3–23). Adonijah got the support of a backslidden priest, for Abiathar was once one of David's counsellors and had stood with David at the time of Absalom's rebellion. Now he abandons David at the time of Adonijah's attempt to steal the throne.

But God's king, David, puts these men down. In the midst of his banqueting, Adonijah suddenly hears the news. His attempt to take over God's kingdom has been put down by one who is more of a king than he is. The king is already riding on David's mule. The trumpet is already blowing for God's king. The people are already rejoicing in King Solomon. Solomon has already taken his seat on the throne. This is how God's kingdom works. When evil and wickedness seem to be triumphing suddenly God acts in power. His people are given victory and triumph.

4. **The kingdom of God offers mercy** (1 Kings 1:50–53). By ancient Israelite standards Adonijah was likely to have been instantly executed. But Solomon offers him mercy. He finds mercy at a place of sacrifice (1:50). He is offered radical and total forgiveness (1:51–52). Yet though he is offered mercy he is also told he must *'go to his home'*. His life as a rebel must come to an end. His opposition to God's man must cease.

It turns out that Adonijah's plea for mercy is fake. Soon he is seeking the kingship again (2:13–24) and as a result he loses his life (2:25). But so far as Solomon is concerned, mercy was offered to Adonijah. Judgement is the result of mercy rejected. God's kings act in mercy. God's kingdom is a kingdom of mercy before it is ever a kingdom of judgement.

'He has made us to be a kingdom' says Revelation 1:6. *'They will reign'* says Revelation 5:10. We *'reign in life'* says Romans 5:17. Jesus is the great King and we are lesser kings under Him. We know what it is to be revived by God's Holy

Spirit. We know what it is to exercise authority and spiritual energy because we are enjoying the anointing of the Holy Spirit. We are able to triumph over opposition. We enjoy reigning with Christ in a kingdom of mercy.

Chapter 3

Delayed Justice
(1 Kings 2:1–25)

David is concerned for the future of the kingdom of God. He knows he will soon be leaving this world and wants to commission his son Solomon and give him some parting words of advice.

1. **Kingship involved God-given strength** (2:1–4). Solomon must look to God for strength, manliness and faithfulness. He must be strong (2:1a). It is a call that is often found in the Scriptures. Solomon is facing the loneliness of being king. He will have to bear heavy responsibilities. He will face opposition. As the king of God's people he has an onerous task.

He has to *'show himself a man'*, an adult (2:2). He has to grow up fast. He is not to be like a child. Children are dependent, double-minded, over-optimistic, pleasure-obsessed. Mature people move on and *'put away childish things'*.

He is to keep the charge of the LORD (2:3). This involves *'walking in His ways'*, following the guidance of His written Word.

This is how Jesus was, strong in His Father, mature in His dependence on God, faithful to what the Father asked of Him. The Christian is given the same advice: be strong in the Lord (Ephesians 6:10). We are kings also. We reign with Jesus. We too have a royal calling, and will face much opposition from the spiritual world.

If Solomon lives this way, his life will be characterised by success. He will see the fulfilment of God's purpose in his life.

2. **Kingship involves justice** (2:5–27). Solomon must look to God to see that his kingdom is made secure by the implementation of justice (2:5–11). There were men in Isreal who had never been truly rewarded or punished for what they had done. Joab's wickedness (2:5–6), Barzillai's loyalty (2:7), and Shimei's arrogance (2:8–9) had never been repaid. They had never reaped the deserts of their ways. David expresses his concern about these matters and then he dies. 2 Samuel 2:10–12 records the end of his reign and the beginning of the reign of Solomon. There is one person omitted from David's remarks about seeing justice done in his kingdom. Adonijah's wickedness was also great and yet David said nothing about him. It was typical of David that although he wanted justice done and the kingdom protected from Joab and Shimei, he said nothing about Adonijah. David could not face the thought of urging justice to be done against his own son.

It may seem suprising that after a lifetime of mercy and generosity to his enemies, David should now be asking that justice should be executed upon Joab and Shimei. Earlier David had been remarkably forgiving concerning Shimei (see 2 Samuel 16:5–12). There was even a time when David protected Shimei against one who wanted him to be executed (see 2 Samuel 19:16–23). Why should he now be giving instructions concerning Joab and Shimei's execution?

The answer surely is that David built forgiveness into his kingdom, with regard to his personal relationships. It was one of the things that made David a man after God's own heart. But now David is about to die, and he knows it. What is on his heart now is not his personal feelings about his enemies, but the justice and the safety of his son's kingdom.

Forgiveness in personal relationships is one thing. The execution of justice and the safety of the kingdom is another thing. In personal relationships David is forgiving. In protection of the kingdom and the administration of justice

David is stern. We are to live at peace with everyone, but the governing authorities do not bear the sword for nothing (Romans 12:18; 13:4).

The principle behind this is that although justice may be delayed, it arrives eventually. Joab had been a ruthless murderer. Shimei had disgracefully insulted and attacked David. Adonijah had planned the overthrow of God's king. All of them seemed to have escaped any kind of judgement falling on them. But this is the way it is with God. Judgement does not always come immediately after the sin. Often a person sins and nothing happens at all. Justice is delayed. David and Jesus are similar. Jesus comes to bring forgiveness. He wants to save, not to judge. Yet judgement comes eventually. Jesus the Saviour will one day be Jesus the Judge.

Adonijah's judgement came when God handed him over to the folly of his own ways. Adonijah had withdrawn his claim to the throne while David was alive but his heart had not changed. He was as ambitious as ever. God sometimes judges sin by handing us over to our own foolishness. So it was with Adonijah. He soon renewed his attempts to get to be the king. He acts cunningly, appealing to one that Solomon was likely to listen to, Bathsheba his mother (2:13–21). His motive was clearly to get to the throne (2:15). He pretends he is content with things as they are (*'It has come to him from the LORD'*, 2:15) but it is obvious that he is insincere. Taking over a previous king's concubine was a way of claiming the throne. He acts as if what he is asking is a small matter, just *'one request'* (2:16). He moves slowly, feeling his way with Bathsheba, avoiding Solomon himself (2:17).

Bathsheba is deceived and believes his claim to peacefulness (2:13). She gives him permission to speak and accepts his request (2:18). She puts the case sympathetically to Solomon (2:19–21). She is gullible. She does not seem to realise that if Adonijah gets his way her own son will lose his throne.

But Solomon is not deceived (2:22) and takes action.

19

Adonijah has given Solomon reason to withdraw the previous offer of mercy. Solomon has reason to execute justice upon Adonijah for his previous rebellion (2:23–25). Mercy had been offered to Adonijah (1:52–53). Instead of making use of Solomon's merciful offer he had clung to his wicked plans, but he only brought justice more swiftly upon himself. Justice is often delayed to give us a chance to amend our ways. But if the opportunity for forgiveness is not taken, sooner or later we shall be handed over to our own foolishness, and will bring our own judgement down upon our heads.

Chapter 4

Justice and Mercy

(1 Kings 2:26–46)

Solomon was told by David to see that Joab and Shimei should be executed and (2:5–6, 8–9) and Barzillai rewarded (2:7). No mention was made of David's son Adonijah or of Abiathar who had been loyal to David but had foolishly chosen the wrong side in an attempted coup. In these verses we see how three men received the results of their wickedness. Presumably Barzillai was also rewarded as David had said (2:7). Not only is justice delayed, reward is delayed also. But eventually Barzillai reaped blessing because of his loyalty to David.

1. **Abiathar discovers the lunacy of jealousy** (2:26–27). Solomon, as a wise king, mixes justice with mercy. Adonijah and Joab are military men and are a danger to the kingdom. Abiathar is an elderly high-priest. It is somewhat surprising that Abiathar had supported Adonijah, for he had long served David and it seems to have been known that it was God's will and David's will that Solomon should be the next king. Apparently Abiathar thought he stood a better chance of promotion in Adonijah's group of rebels. Solomon shows Abiathar mercy. He is sent to his family home at Anathoth with the understanding that if he is no danger to Solomon he will be allowed to live. Yet Solomon's words *I will not put you to death at this time* (2:26) hint that he will be dealt with severely if there is any sign of rebellion. It is a last chance. Presumably he remained there at peace; nothing more is

heard of him. Jeremiah was descended from *'one of the priests at Anathoth'* (Jeremiah 1:1) and so may have come from his family.

What brought about Abiathar's disloyalty? It was rivalry with Zadok. Jealousy will lead to foolish decisions being made. Both Abiathar and Zadok were candidates for the office of high priest. Abiathar apparently thought he had a better chance of power in high office if he joined the side of an attempted take-over of Solomon's kingdom. But rivalry and jealousy were Abiathar's downfall. After a lifetime of loyalty he threw everything away because of jealousy. Solomon treated him with mercy but he never regained his usefulness in God's kingdom.

2. **Joab finds that religiosity will not help him** (2:28–35). Joab knows that his life is in danger and runs to the tabernacle to cling to the altar as a place of safety. It would be nice to think that this was his clinging to the place of atonement in the hour of death. If so it would mean that he found salvation in his dying hours, despite a lifetime's murderous habits. But the truth is there was no 'altar-asylum' in Israel, although there was in the surrounding pagan nations. The law of Moses actually said that if a murderer ran to the altar *'You shall take him even from mine altar that He may die'* (Deuteronomy 19:12). Disregarding God's word on the matter, Joab was clinging to a pagan superstition that surrounding nations believed in but which was not allowed in Israel. To have gone straight to God for mercy was what was needed. *'You do not delight in sacrifice'*, said David who was also a murderer, *'or I would bring it. The sacrifices of God are a broken spirit'* (Psalm 51:16, 17). David did not turn to religion; he turned to God. Joab did not turn to God; he turned to religion. David found mercy, Joab did not.

3. **Shimei discovers that one exception to the rule can be fatal**. Mercy is offered to Shimei (2:36–46). David had urged that Shimei should receive the punishment of his sin and yet had told Solomon to deal with him in wisdom (2:8–9). He was offered release from the consequences of

what he had done on condition that he stayed in Jerusalem. If he crossed the Kidron valley (just outside Jerusalem) he could expect execution (2:36–37). However Shimei soon found himself in a situation where he thought he could break Solomon's ruling without any harm coming to himself (2:38–40). He lost his life through his refusing to keep to Solomon's ruling (2:41–46).

Often when we know God's will we think that one small exception will do no harm. Solomon was king and had given a clear word to Shimei. *'On the day when you cross the Kidron you will die'* Solomon had said. But Shimei had lost some slaves. He felt he had special reason to make this time an 'exception to the rule'. It is the way we often reason in our foolishness. Some situation arises and we feel that we can make this an 'exception to the rule'. 'We'll go over Kidron just this once', we say. 'I would not normally do it, but this is a special situation'. 'I don't think the King would mind this one occasion'. But Shimei found that making oneself the exception to the rule can be disastrous. His one exception to Solomon's ruling brought his life to an end.

4. **Solomon discovered that the way of patient wisdom is the way of success**. The end result of the events of these early years in Solomon's reign was that *'The kingdom was now firmly established in Solomon's hands'* (2:46). He had mixed boldness with caution. Joab and Adonijah were immediate threats and were removed boldly and swiftly. Shimei and Abiathar were not so dangerous and Solomon had not taken action against them in a impulsive manner but had waited for events to mature. Now Solomon is in a strong position. He has behind him the tradition he has inherited from David. Prosperity and national loyalty are on his side. God was with him. *'Solomon sat on the throne of the LORD as king ... he prospered ... all Israel obeyed him ... the LORD highly exalted him and bestowed on his royal majesty'* (1 Chronicles 29:23–25). He himself had already learned that patient wisdom brought better results than Adonijah's manipulativeness or Shimei's self-centredness

or Joab's careless violence. His heart was tender. His gifts were great. His advantages were many. The New Testament refers to *'Solomon in all his glory'*. The question is: what will he do with his great advantages?

Chapter 5

Wisdom and Folly

(1 Kings 3:1–28)

Solomon was a man born with many advantages. He had grown up in the palace and had known wealth from his earliest days. His parents were David and Bathsheba, whose marriage had been overruled for good and was a strong and longlasting marriage. From his earliest days Solomon had known that God had plans to use him. He had a good relationship with his parents. Of all of David's sons, only Solomon liked to talk of 'my father'. He had also three brothers (1 Chronicles 3:5).

Solomon was never a man of war. Unlike his father, he never fought a bear or a lion, never fought with a Goliath. Instead he wrote books, like parts of Proverbs and the Song of Songs.

He came to faith in the God of Israel at a young age and became a man of God. We find him dedicating himself to God (3:4–15) and his prayer at the temple was the prayer of a godly man (8:12–61). He had David's talent for administration, and so his reign was a time of successful trade with surrounding nations, and of growth within the nation. Solomon was especially successful as a builder of buildings.

We need to know about kingship. Not only is Jesus a King above all kings, but also the Christian reigns with Christ. The book of kings shows us how few were the kings who measured up to the standard of kingship that David had set. Only Jesus could qualify as a true 'Son of David'. But we can learn much from the various successes and failures of those who followed in the line of David.

In the case of Solomon we see from the earliest beginnings of his reign that he is a mixture of silliness and wisdom. He is known for his wisdom but there is foolishness in him also, even from his first days.

1. **Solomon was foolish in the friendships he made**. Our reigning with Christ will be hindered by foolishness. Other than our Lord Jesus Christ, no one ever shows pure and undiluted wisdom. We are all a mixture of folly and wisdom. We need to learn to reduce our folly and increase our wisdom. Solomon's story shows us his foolishness before it shows us his wisdom.

Solomon made a bad mistake in using marriage to make a political alliance. It was fitting that he should be friendly to a nearby powerful country, Egypt. He was a king, and he had to relate to kingdoms that were nearby. It was sensible to be friendly to them. But Solomon went too far. He was already married with a son when he first became king (see 1 Kings 11:42–43 with 14:21). Now he was eager to make alliances with surrounding nations, and this led him into marrying a pagan princess (3:1). The reason was political. He wanted to have a strong nation with good relationships with surrounding nations, and this was the way such alliances were generally made. A king would marry a neighbouring king's daughter. The Pharaoh was one called Siamun, although he is not given a name in the Bible. Solomon was wise but he was foolish as well! Strong alliances with Egypt and marriage to Pharaoh's daughter might seem politically wise but it was spiritually dangerous. Solomon perhaps knew this. He did not make his pagan wife his top priority (3:2), for he built the temple, the wall of Jerusalem, and his palace before attending to her needs. Yet eventually Israel would be ruined by alliances with paganism.

Christians should be friendly to everyone, but our deepest friendships need to be with God's people. To marry an unbeliever will generally lead to disaster. It will redirect one's future into ways of suffering and perhaps into ways of sin.

2. **Solomon was foolish in tolerating the 'high places'** (3:2). These were open-air places of worship. Some were used for worship of the God of Israel, like the one at Gibeon, but there were many where the worship was corrupt and idolatrous.

3. **Foolishness and sincerity may be combined in God's servant.** So it was with Solomon. Although there are indications of foolishness in the story we are being told, yet we are also told that he *'loved the Lord'* and followed in the godly ways of his father David. So we are told of his godliness and sincerity combined (1 Kings 3:3). Even godly men have blemishes.

4. **Our reigning with Christ is helped by wisdom.** Solomon's godly sinceriy as a young man led him into ways of wisdom even before God gave him an added gift of wisdom. We see his wisdom in his dedication of himself to God (3:4). God honoured him by speaking to him (3:5). To him that has shall more be given. If we make good use of the wisdom we have God will give us more.

We see his wisdom in his humility (3:6). As he was praying he saw he was dependent on God (3:6), and God was honouring David's faithfulness. He admitted his lack of experience (3:7), and saw how great his responsibility was (3:8). He showed great wisdom in asking for more wisdom (3:9).

God honoured his prayer (3:10). He was pleased Solomon did not ask for long life, or wealth, or revenge (3:11). So Solomon's prayer was answered (3:12). If we seek first God's kingdom, other needs will be met. God gives Solomon even the things he had not asked for (3:13). He also makes an offer to him. If he will continue in godliness he will live for a long time (3:14).

5. **Opportunity will come to us to use the gifts God has given us.** Solomon soon found himself in a situation where it became clear that God had given him a gift of wisdom. Two women had recently given birth to two children, but one of

the children had died. There is a suspicion that one has perhaps stolen the child of the other (1 Kings 3:16–22). The king listens carefully (3:23) and finds a way of discerning the motives of their hearts (3:24–26). His gift becomes known. God will sooner or later bring any gift we have into the situation where it is needed.

Chapter 6

Wisdom in the Nation
(1 Kings 4:1–34)

Solomon had sought and had received a miraculous gift of wisdom from God. Wisdom is not the same as knowledge. There are plenty of people who are knowledgeable but lack wisdom. Many young students grow in knowledge without growing in wisdom. Wisdom may **use** knowledge but it is not exactly the same as knowledge. Wisdom is largely a matter of skill in getting things done. It is practical know-how in the things of God. Its beginning is the fear of the Lord (Proverbs 1:7).

Solomon was famous for his wisdom and we see all the ingredients of true wisdom in his life.

1. **Wisdom begins with the fear of the Lord** (see Proverbs 1:7). Solomon had this basic fear of the Lord as we can see in the early events of his life (see 3:4–15).

2. **Wisdom involves skill in discernment and decision-making**. This has also been displayed in Solomon's life (3:16–28).

Now 1 Kings 4 brings us to two other aspects of wisdom.

3. **Wisdom involves skill in administration** (4:1–28). When a man or woman is given wisdom, he will soon be given responsibility. Then when the area over which he is responsible grows he will need assistants. He will need to cooperate with people. His wisdom is then tested as to whether he is skilful in discerning who should be his colleagues, and whether he is able to cope in relating to people. Handling

things or machines or papers is one thing. Skill at organising people is another. Machines do as they are told, most of the time! But people get offended when handled tactlessly. People have prejudices and opinions of their own. Machines and papers behave themselves according to how they are programmed but people are sinners. One of the greatest aspects of Solomon's wisdom and gifting was the fact that he could handle large-scale administration.

Wise administration involves *the choice of colleagues* (4:1–6). Many of Solomon's officials were known to him as those who had been in the service of his father. His chief officials included Azariah (4:2, a 'son', actually grandson, of Zadok, who was a priest in David's time, 2 Samuel 15:29, 36), two brothers who were given high office as adminstrators (4:3), Jehoshaphat (who also had served under David, 2 Samuel 8:16), Benaiah who had proved his skill and loyalty as a soldier in the days of David, and two sons of Nathan. (Nathan may have been the prophet, but there was also a son of David called Nathan, 2 Samuel 5:14–15). Adoniram (or Adoram) had also worked for David (2 Samuel 20:24). It is clear that Solomon chose experienced men and men who were known to him. His choice of colleagues was careful and wise.

Wise administration involves *sub-dividing responsibility* (4:7–19). No one can run a work of God on his own. Solomon could not rule Israel alone. The more thoroughly he administered his country, the more thoroughly he needed to sub-divide and allocate smaller units of reponsibility. So he divided the land into twelve and appointed twelve 'District Governors'. Of the twelve districts mentioned in 1 Kings 4:7–19 some of them were roughly the same as the areas of particular tribes but they incorporated into them areas captured from surrounding foreign peoples.

Wise administration involves *maintaining peace from the centre outwards* (4:20–28). The people of Israel entered into great prosperity at this time. To eat, drink and rejoice (4:20) is an Old Testament way of speaking of contentment and harmony. The land flourished socially and economically under Solomon's rule. Its borders were enlarged (4:21).

At the heart of the régime was the palace. Solomon took care that this administrative centre received abundant provision. Flour and meal were needed (4:22). Cattle, sheep, goats and other animals were necessary for the daily meals at the palace with its large staff (4:23). The palace was the administrative centre of a large empire (4:24). From this well-maintained centre, peace and prosperity streamed out into the empire. There was peace *'from all who passed through his land from the surounding areas'* (as 4:24 is best translated). It was not a total peace throughout the whole reign (see 11:14, 23, 26) but it controlled travellers (4:24), and provided safety throughout the territory. Each family had a plot of land so as to be able to enjoy the fertility of the country (4:25). The prosperity of the entire country contributed to the well-being of the centre, and the prosperity of the palace was geared to ministering to the country.

This wisdom had, as we have seen, strands of folly in it. Verse 26 tells of Solomon's cavalry. He had four thousand[1] sets of horses, grouped in twos and threes to pull chariots, and twelve thousand riders of chariots. Yet one thing the Mosaic law said about kings was that they should not accumulate horses! Verses 27–28 bring the section to an end, speaking of provision for Solomon (4:27) and provision for his horses (4:28)!

4. **Wisdom involves accumulation and documentation of knowledge** (4:29–34). Solomon evidently sponsored great accumulations of factual knowledge. Wisdom does not consist in pure knowledge but wisdom needs to make use of knowledge (4:29). Solomon's wisdom of this kind outstripped the wisdom of surrounding nations (4:30–31).

This wisdom also produced literature. The Old Testament book of Proverbs has at least 582 of Solomon's proverbs. Solomon evidently created parks and gardens (see Ecclesiastes 2:5) and used them to make practical examination of various aspects of nature. The result was a body of literature making use of observations made in Solomon's parks

(4:32–34). All of this is part of wisdom. Peace in a nation leads to science, and science in the hands of wisdom leads to practical handbooks for the life of the people.

5. **Wisdom promoted the prosperity of the nation**. It had a happy influence upon every aspect of national life. Godliness has many practical side-effects. Where there is godly wisdom God's people are encouraged, commerce, scholarship and learning are advanced, literature becomes elevated and pure, peaceful relationships with surrounding nations are maintained. All of this took place under Solomon. The fear of the Lord was the beginning of his wisdom; national prosperity was its outcome.

Yet all of this also had within it the seeds of decay. Solomon's strands of foolishness would grow but his wisdom would be ignored. In the story of 1 and 2 Kings we shall find all of this crumbling. The seeds of false religion that Solomon sowed were to grow. The customs of pagan nations would increasingly take over the godly culture of Solomon. Despotism would arise within the nation. It would break the nation into two, Israel and Judah. First Israel in the north and then Judah in the south would be overrun by enemies. Jerusalem itself would be destroyed. The prosperity of Israel was built up through its godliness in the reign of Solomon but it would be lost through its ungodliness in the following centuries. It was Solomon himself who said it: righteousness exalts a nation but sin is a reproach.

Today, where the gospel of Jesus gets a hold upon sufficiently large numbers of people, and where godly wisdom is brought into the nation, it will have side-effects which slowly gather momentum in the life of the state. Yet it will never be perfect in this world. It seems that nations will always ebb and flow in their prosperity. Solomon's prosperity contained seeds of destruction within it. Wheat and weeds grow alongside each other while the world lasts. When Jesus a greater than Solomon appears, weeds will be burned up and a Solomonic glory will again take hold of this world in Jesus.

Footnote

[1] There are tricky points of translation here. (i) **Forty** is a slip that arose in the copying of the Hebrew manuscript; it should be 'four' (as is found in the old Greek translation and in 2 Chronicles 9:25). (ii) The Hebrew refers not to 'stalls' (NIV) but to horses stabled together in groups of twos or threes. (iii) There is a Hebrew word here which means either 'horses' or 'horses and riders'.

Chapter 7

Preparing for the Temple
(1 Kings 5:1–18)

1 Kings 5:1 to 9:14 is concerned with the two major building projects of Solomon which took twenty years to complete. The section begins and ends with mention of Hiram (5:1–12; 9:10–14). We are told of a treaty with Hiram (1 Kings 5:1–12) and of Solomon's massive work force (5:13–18). Solomon was taking risks in both of these matters and both of these aspects of his wisdom were to have harmful consequences in later days.

1. **Solomon made use of the skills of the world**. Friendship came easily to him. He had admirers *'from all the kings of the earth'* (4:34). Hiram took the initiative in the friendship, making a friendly move at the time Solomon became king (5:1). Solomon replied telling Hiram the story of his wish to build a temple (5:2–4), and that he was now intending to fulfil a longstanding plan (5:5). He asked the Sidonian king to provide help (5:6). Hiram was happy to respond (5:7–9) and a good relationship between the kings began (5:10–11). It was part of Solomon's 'wisdom' to have made a good treaty with Hiram (5:12).

Solomon had a good trading partner in Hiram. The Phoenicians of Tyre provided labourers and materials for Solomon's temple, especially Lebanese wood. They designed his ships and provided sailors for him. They were a market for Israelite products such as wheat and olive oil.

Hiram's friendship was useful to Solomon both politically and practically. One cannot say that it was in itself sinful.

There is a 'worldly' side even to the work of God. The temple was to be a dwelling-place in which God would reveal himself. Yet it required Phoenician material and Phoenician workmen for it to be built! This was not in any way sinful although it had its dangers. The Christian lives in this world. He does business. He buys and sells goods. He employs builders, perhaps. His children may go to government schools. He may need the attention of a doctor, a dentist, a garage mechanic. Not all of these people will be believing people and yet the Christian has contact with them and organises his life with their help. Christian distinctiveness is not withdrawal from the world.

However there are dangers that our contact with unbelieving people will draw us too far into relationships that are too intimate, so much so that our lives become corrupted. One needs to maintain a balance and be aware of one's own weaknesses. Solomon himself seems to have been one of those people who will do anything to please an ally, and who will get drawn into sin because of his friendships. Solomon's ability to win friends and influence people led him into compromise. Josephus the Jewish historian tells us that Solomon married Hiram's daughter. It is probably true. Certainly 1 Kings 11:1 mentions Sidonians among the women he married. Presumably they were the result of his friendly relationship with Hiram the Sidonian. 'Sidonian' was another name for Phoenician. Tyre and Sidon were famous Phoenician cities. Building a good relationship with Hiram was wisdom; marrying Sidonian women was folly. Even in the building of the temple, strands of wisdom and foolishness can be seen intertwined in Solomon's life.

2. **Solomon created a system of compulsory labour for the nation**. He introduced a system of 'national service' in order to get the temple built (5:13–14). It was less demanding for Israelites and more demanding for immigrants. There were thirty thousand Israelite recruits but at any one time only ten thousand were serving in Lebanon; the other twenty

thousand were allowed to be at home. So they were engaged in work for the nation for four months of the year.

Solomon also introduced a form of slavery which made use of tens of thousands of non-Israelite workers (5:15). This was much heavier work and they were treated more harshly than their Israelite colleagues, since there was no eight months per year freedom for them. Another 3,300 Israelite overseers were also employed (5:16). With this large labour force at work the foundation-stone of the temple was laid (5:17). Solomon's men and Hiram's men, aided by Gebalites, skilful workers from a Phoenician town called Gebal, prepared the stones and the timber for the building (5:18).

Once again, all of this was the beginning of something that was to cause trouble in days to come. It takes great skill to mobilize such a work-force without inspiring bitterness. Solomon prevailed in getting his wishes done but at the end of his reign people complained to his son, *'Your father made our yoke heavy'* and pleaded *'lighten the hard labour that he imposed on us'* (1 Kings 12:4). When Rehoboam replied harshly the kingdom of Israel broke into two.

All of this reminds us of the limitations of holy buildings. The entire project was an earthly matter.

What was this 'temple' all about? It was the place where God *'put his name'* (Deuteronomy 12:5) and had as His dwelling-place (Deuteronomy 12:5). It would become the supreme central sanctuary for the entire nation (Deuteronomy 12:5–28). Deuteronomy had predicted that its site and its building could not be chosen and consecrated until Israel had thoroughly finished its work of conquering the land of Canaan and had been given 'rest' in the land (Deuteronomy 12:8–11). Such rest only came in the days of David (2 Samuel 7:1) and was being enjoyed in the days of Solomon (1 Kings 5:3–4; 8:56). A *'house for the Lord's name'* could not be built till then (1 Kings 3:2; 8:16).

Its site was the threshing floor of Araunah (2 Samuel 24), the place where the fire fell to ignite David's offering (1 Chronicles 21:26; 22:1). It is also identified with Mount

Moriah, the place where Abraham was willing to *'spare not his own son'* (2 Chronicles 3:1; see Genesis 22:2, 14).

Many of the materials had been collected by David (1 Chronicles 18:8) and many details had been planned by him (1 Chronicles 22–26). Its structure was a matter of divine revelation. Solomon had a plan *'in writing from the hand of the Lord'* (1 Chronicles 28:11–19).

In the book of psalms we discover how much the tabernacle and temple meant to the Israelites. *'I love the house where you live ... the place where your glory dwells'* said David, referring to the pre-Solomonic tabernacle (Psalm 26:8). *'I long to dwell in your tent'*, he said on another occasion (Psalm 61:4). And on another occasion, *'We are filled with the good things of your house, of your holy sanctuary'* (Psalm 65:4).

The psalmists delight in God's house. It is God's dwelling-place (Psalm 84:1), a place to travel to on pilgrimage (Psalm 84:5). Better one day in the courts of the Lord than a thousand elsewhere (Psalm 84:10). They speak in loving terms of the *'house'*, the *'holy hill'*. They long to journey to Jerusalem where the tabernacle was in David's day, later to be replaced by the temple. *'Let us go to the house of the Lord'* is their hearts' desire (Psalm 122:1). They are unhappy when they cannot get there (Psalm 42:1–4; compare Jonah 2:4). It is the *'holy mountain'*, the *'place where you dwell'*, the place where they know the altar is, and where God is their joy and their delight (Psalm 43:3–4). In its courts they pay their vows, bring their offerings, worship God and behold His beauty. In its courts they fasted in times of crisis, and listened to God's prophets. The psalmist asked *'How can I repay the Lord for all his goodness?'* (Psalm 116:12) and went to the house of God to fulfil his vows amidst the crowds of others doing the same (Psalm 116:14). In the courts of the tabernacle or temple he would bring sacrifices of gratitude (Psalm 116:17–19).

It must be remembered however that no ordinary Israelite could go inside the temple. Its rooms were reserved for the priests and only the high-priest of the nation could enter the holy of holies. All of this must be taken by the Christian in a **spiritual** way. The earthly building of the temple was important only as the expression of worship and gratitude and enjoyment of the Lord's presence. The people who understood the significance of the temple the most were the friends of Stephen, a Greek-speaking believer. It was Stephen more than any other (before Paul) who realised that Mosaic law was terminated when Jesus came and the system of temple worship and animal sacrifice was fulfilled and terminated in Jesus. Stephen knew that the tabernacle had been made as directed by God (Acts 7:44) and that it had been replaced by the temple (Acts 7:47). Yet he also knew that the temple was not God's true and final dwelling-place (7:48). Following Stephen the writers of the New Testament teach that the temple finds **spiritual** fulfilment in a **spiritual** temple, the people of God, with **spiritual** sacrifices (Romans 12:1; Hebrews 13:15–16; 1 Peter 2:5).

Chapter 8

A Place for God's Name
(1 Kings 6:1–13)

God planned to put His name or 'glory' in the temple. He said *'I will put my name there'* (1 Kings 3:2; 8:16–20, 29; 9:23).

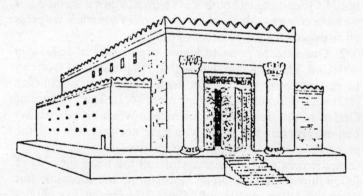

God's name is His glory, His holy presence radiating out. Sometimes this glory was only known by faith, but inside the Holy of Holies, it would have been visible to the naked eye, except that generally speaking no one could go there. It would kill any person to see the glory of God directly. When the high-priest went there once a year, a cloud of incense stopped him from being able to see the glory of God.

There is no literal temple-building nowadays. But God's temple in ancient Israel teaches us some things about the presence of God. There are three things that are mentioned as being God's temple in the New Testament: (i) the body of Jesus (John 2:21); (ii) the church, the fellowship of believers (1 Corinthians 3:16; Ephesians 2:22; Hebrews 3:6; 1 Peter 2:5; 2 Corinthians 6:16); and (iii) individual believers are God's temples. In 1 Corinthians 6:19 Paul said to the Corinthians *'Your body is a temple of the Holy Spirit'*.

Eight principles are noticeable in the structure of the temple here in these verses.

1. **Our need of the presence of God**. The date (6:1) tells us of the importance of experiencing the presence of God. It was twelve generations after the exodus (480 years although the figure is apparently not literal)[1]. The building of the temple was an event as important as the deliverance from Egypt. God redeemed His people by the blood of the lamb, but His long-term purpose was to dwell among them. After we have come to salvation *'by the blood of the lamb'* we press on to **experience** the presence of God.

2. **Our need to press to higher experiences of fellowship with God**. The structure tells us that the presence of God can be progressively known. The temple had a main building (6:2) with a 'porch', a front entrance (6:3). The presence of God was progressively experienced. When (symbolically) you are entering the porch, you have not yet come into the presence of God, but you are getting near. In the first compartment you are nearer still and there are symbols of fellowship there (the bread, the lamps, the incense). But when you are in the holy of holies – still speaking symbolically – you are experiencing the presence of God in the highest degree.

The basic dimensions (6:2–3) are given. The length and breadth were sixty and twenty cubits. (A cubit was about 17.5 inches.) It becomes clear that the temple was divided into two rooms (see 6:16, 17). The height was thirty cubits. At the front of this area was a porch whose width was the same as the rest of the buildings (twenty cubits). It extended ten cubits further forward at the front of the building. *'And the entrance hall in front of the main room of the house was 20 cubits, the same as the breadth; and ten cubits was its measurement forward in front of the house'* (6:3).

This means that the buildings basic structure was three-fold. There was a porch, a main hall and an innermost sanctuary.

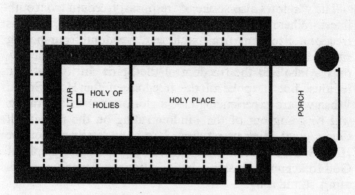

All of this was symbolism. No one except the priests went into the holy place, and no one except the high priest went into the holy of holies. The temple was quite small. It was not a meeting place. It was a dwelling place for God's visible glory. It was also prophetic, because it was only after the coming of Jesus that rich experiences of enjoying God's presence could be known by the whole of God's people. Before then it was known only to a few who had a forward-looking faith in the coming of a Saviour.

3. **Our need of unhurried care in worship**. The porch spoke of care and preparation for worship. The priest was not allowed to step straight from the outside world into the holy inside rooms of the temple. Before he stepped into the temple there was the porch lined with gold reminding the priest that he was doing something sacred and serious in approaching the presence of God.

4. **The importance of prayer and of the Holy Spirit**. The windows are described next (6:4).[2] They were placed high in

43

the walls, so it was not possible to look in through them. They did two things. They let the incense out and they let fresh air in. Incense speaks of prayer. The high-priest symbolically prayed when he burnt incense and clouds of sweet-smelling perfume went up towards the sky. Our praying is mixed with the praying of the High-priest, Jesus.

The windows also spoke of freshness, freedom from stuffiness. Where the presence of God is experienced, there is freedom. Freedom from stuffiness, freedom from boring ritual, freedom from endless repetition. Of course the law only **symbolised** the freedom of the Spirit. In itself it was tedious. But it spoke of the freedom of the Holy Spirit. When we are experiencing God's glorious presence, prayers will be going out of the window riding on the prayers of God's great High-priest Jesus. And the 'fresh air' of the Holy Spirit will constantly be coming into the temple of God to keep it refreshing, invigorating, energising, exhilarating, stimulating.

5. **The effects of the presence of God**. There were rooms built on the side of the temple (6:5–6) but they were not part of the temple itself. The side wings spoke of the fact that the life of the temple would be highly productive. There would be people to be accommodated, treasures to be stored. All of these required extra rooms. They were not part of the temple itself, but they were built around the temple.

6. **The peace of the presence of God**. The work of building the temple was done without excessive noise. Iron tools were not allowed on the site (6:7). The temple was to be a place of peace, so nothing that disturbed the peace was allowed. The presence of God brings peace, not the peace of an easy life, but the peace of knowing that we are right with God and are enjoying God's presence. The temple had within it the place of sacrifice, the place of atonement for sin. Where we are enjoying reconciliation with God, we have peace. Nor could activities in the side-rooms disturb the temple. The description of the entrances and stairs (6:8) shows that the store-rooms could not be entered from inside the temple.

7. **The strength of the presence of God**. Next comes mentions of the basic features that involve wood. The roof involved beams of cedar woods (6:9) and the supports outside the building holding the extra rooms were also built of cedar wood (6:10). The temple had strong wooden girders in it to give it strength. The presence of God gives strength and stability, so it was only right that the house for His presence should not be something likely to collapse. It was built to last a long time.

8. **The call to obedience**. Now that the basic description has been given (6:1–10) next comes mention of a word from God (6:11–13). Apparently it came to Solomon at this point. The basic structure had been built but before the project proceeded to the inside fittings and furnishings Solomon was given a warning. The indwelling of God among His people would be conditional upon the obedience of the king. (The word 'you' is singular.)

After we have been *'redeemed by the blood of the lamb'* we are to want to be temples for God. The more God's presence is with us the more we shall experience His peace, His strength, His radiating holiness in our lives, His strength. But such an experience of His obvious and radiating presence in our lives will be dependent upon obedience. In Solomon's case it required obedience to the Mosaic law: in our case it will mean obedience to the Holy Spirit. We are God's house **if** we hold fast to confident obedient faith (Hebrews 3:6).

Footnotes

[1] The actual date of the exodus seems to have been about 1240 BC and the date of the temple was some time round about 967 BC so the distance between the two was about 280 years. Unless there is a textual slip (in which 480 was read for 280) the date must be an artificial one, in which a generation was considered to be forty years.

[2] The Hebrew of this verse is difficult. It has been taken to mean 'with recessed frames' (RSV) or to lattice-work.

Chapter 9

Paradise Restored

(1 Kings 6:14–38)

1. **The presence of God is paradise restored**. 1 Kings 6:15 describes the inside of the entire building. It had a pinewood floor and cedarwood for the ceilings and walls. *'Then he built the walls of the house on the inside with boards of cedar; from the floor of the house to the ceiling he overlaid the walls on the inside with wood, and he overlaid the floor of the house with boards of cypress'*. No stone could be seen at all.

Verses 16 and 17 describe a partition of cedarwood inside the temple, twenty cubits from the rear wall. So the temple was divided inside into two rooms by a wooden wall. *'And he built twenty cubits in the rear part of the house with boards of cedar from the floor to the ceiling. He built for it on the inside, for a sanctuary, for a holy of holies. And forty cubits was the house, that is, the main hall in front of it'*.

Verse 18 describes the woodwork done in the holy of holies. Carved on the walls were carvings of gourds (large hard-skinned fruits) and open flowers. *'And the cedar on the house within was carved with pomegranates and open flowers. The whole was cedar; there was no stone visible'*.

The inside of the temple was not to be a typical building like other buildings. It was unlike other buildings. It was designed in such a way that you could not see the internal stonework. When the priest was inside the temple he could not see anything that made him conscious he was inside a stone building. Rather the inside of the temple seems to have been the model of a garden. What was pictured on its walls were representations of gourds and flowers.

What all of this means is that for the priest who did his work inside the temple, it was as though he were back in the garden of Eden. The presence of God is paradise restored. God originally made a garden (Genesis 2:8–9a) and put the human race in it (Genesis 2:15). Man was excluded from the presence of God by sin (Genesis 3:23–24). The temple taught that there was a way back into fellowship with God by the blood of sacrifice. When we are saved we come inside God's temple and are priests enjoying fellowship with God. Revelation 2:7 says *'To him who overcomes, I will give the right to eat from the tree of life which is in the paradise of God'*.

2. **We are to seek the highest degree of restful fellowship with God**. The most wonderful part of the temple was the holy of holies. Verse 16 mentions the inner sanctuary which was like the holy of holies in the tabernacle. It symbolised a high degree of restful fellowship. Verse 17 mentions the larger hall which was equivalent to the holy place of the tabernacle. It symbolised approaching God by means of fellowship with Him.

Verse 19 states the purpose of the inner sanctuary. The holy of holies was designed to receive the ark (6:19), which was the symbol of God's presence. Verse 20a states the dimensions of the holy of holies. It was a perfect cube ($20 \times 20 \times 20$ cubits), which implies that either the floor was raised or there was an internal ceiling (or both), because the height of the main hall was 30 cubits. It seems likely that there were some steps up into it and that it had an internal ceiling lower than the rest of the building. The 'cubical' or 'foursquare' nature of the presence of God points to the nature of the gospel of Jesus. The heavenly Jerusalem of the book of Revelation is also foursquare or cubical. It speaks of the perfection of the gospel. It is rich and full. It meets every need of humankind with perfect balance. It is like the length and depth and width of the love of God (Ephesians 3:18).

3. **The enjoyment of God's presence is life's most valuable blessing**. Verse 20b–22 tells us of the gold in the holy of holies. Its floors and walls and ceilings were overlaid with gold (6:20b). In it was a cedarwood altar also overlaid with gold (6:20). Verse 21 reads *'And Solomon overlaid the inside of the house* (i.e. the holy of holies) *with pure gold and he placed chains of gold across the front of the inner sanctuary; and he overlaid it with gold.* (verse 22) *'And the whole house he overlaid with gold until all the house was finished. Also the whole altar which was that belonged to the sanctuary he overlaid with gold'*. The altar was the altar that burnt incense.

Gold was everywhere inside the holy of holies. The holy of holies stood for the highest form of worship.

4. **The enjoyment of God's presence brings adoration and readiness to live for God**. Inside the holy of holies were also two cherubs (or, to use the Hebrew plural, cherubim), made of olive-wood but covered with gold (6:23–28). They were angelic creatures. Their outstretched wings represented worship and readiness to move at the bidding of their king. They filled the holy of holies with the wings touching the walls.

5. **There is only one way into God's presence**. 1 Kings 6:29–35 consider the house as a whole including the main hall as well as the sanctuary. *'On the walls all around he carved engravings with pictures of cherubs, palm-trees and and open flowers, on the inside and outside. (30) And the floor of the house he overlaid with gold, in the inner room and in the outer room. (31) For the entrance of the inner room he made doors of olive-wood, the frame, that is the doorposts, being five-sided'* (6:31; a coin from Byblos shows a fivesided door in a Phoenician temple.) Verse 32: *'And upon the two doors of olive-wood he made on them carvings of cherubs and palm-trees and open flowers. And he overlaid them with gold. And he thinly coated gold upon the cherubs and upon the palm trees. (33) And so he made for the entrance of the temple doorposts of olive-wood from a fourth. (34) And the two doors he made of cypress-wood, the two leaves of the one door having*

The folding doors of the temple.

hinges to enable them to fold into two. (35) *And he carved cherubs and palm-trees and open flowers; and he overlaid them with gold evenly applied over the carved work'* (6:35).

So we have here the doors, the carvings, and the gold coverings. From the doors one learns that it was possible for the priests to enter into the presence of God, but there was only one way to enter. There was only one way through from outside to the Holy Place, and only one way through into the Holy of Holies. As before the carvings reminded the priests who saw them of a garden. Fellowship with God is paradise restored. The gold coverings spoke of exceedingly great value.

6. **The people who enjoy God's presence are a unique people**. Around the temple building were two courts, an inner court and an outer court. 1 Kings mentions only the

inner of the two. *'And he built the inner court, with three layers of cut stone and a layer of cedar boards'* (6:36). The reference is to a wall with different layers of material. Only the priests were allowed in the inner court. So the court had the effect of marking off the distinctiveness of the temple; it was holy ground compared to its surroundings. Similarly the church of Jesus Christ is a holy people, marked off by God as utterly distinct from the world.

We are told how a foundation was laid in the month Ziv (6:37) and it was finished in the month Bul in the 11th year of Solomon's reign (6:38). From that point on the temple would be a permanent reminder that God's glory was with His people. We recall that the temple finds fulfilment in a spiritual temple, the people of God, with spiritual sacrifices (Romans 12:1; Hebrews 13:15–16; 1 Peter 2:5). It too has a unique foundation, Jesus the Son of God.

Chapter 10

The Palace and the Temple

(1 Kings 7:1–22)

Near to the temple were some other houses, a court for Solomon to do the work of a king, a private apartment for himself, and something similar for his wife (7:1–12). The Palace of the Forest of Lebanon was where Solomon himself was to live. The temple was a house for God's glory. The Palace of the Forest of Lebanon was more directly for himself and tells us of the concerns that were on his heart at this time. He was concerned to put God first because he built the temple first and finished it more speedily. His own home came second and he was not in so much of a hurry (7:1).

We are told of its basic dimensions (7:2), and the main details concerning its walls, ceilings, windows, doors and porch (7:3–6). Four of Solomon's concerns are visible.

1. **He was concerned about justice** and built a *'Hall of Pillars'* (7:7) as a central court where he might sit in judgement to deal with difficult cases that arose in his kingdom. From the earliest days of his reign he had been concerned to see fairness in his kingdom (3:11) and still this was his view of what being a king involved.

2. **He was concerned for his private home**. He built a place that was particularly for himself (7:8a) and a place that was specially for his wife (7:8b). Apparently he wanted both for himself and for his wife, the daughter of Pharaoh, a place where he was able to have some privacy and be free from

the pressures that would arise in the palace. Every servant of God needs privacy of some kind, no matter how crowded may be his circumstances. Everyone needs time to think, time to consider things unhurriedly, time to pray.

3. **Solomon was building not only for himself but for the future**. It is clear from the costly stones that were used (7:9–11) that he was building something that should last for a long time. Every Christian should want to have an impact for good that will last beyond his lifetime.

4. **The king was concerned to have the different areas of life clearly marked out** (7:12). The different aspects of our lives flow into each other. A fragmented and compartmentalised life leads to hypocrisy, the kind of hypocrisy that does not want to 'mix religion and business'. Yet on the other hand it is important to think clearly and have different areas of life clearly marked. Solomon takes a balanced position. The temple and the palace were near each other. His concerns for God's glory and his concerns for his own work were side-by-side. Yet on the other hand Solomon put enclosures around the temple and another enclosure around 'the great court', the House of the Forest of Lebanon. He used the same building technique as was mentioned in 6:36. So the 'great court' of the House of the Forest of Lebanon was clearly marked. Solomon wanted its character to be protected. Equally he wanted the temple to be clearly marked as God's temple (7:12). The concerns of life flow into one another, and yet we preserve the character of the different aspects of God's calling.

The writer has mentioned the basic buildings first (6:1–7:12). Now he comes back to the deal with fuller details concerning the temple. So 1 Kings 7:13–50 brings us back to the temple again, to tell us of the furnishings inside the temple.

1. **Well-chosen colleagues may forward God's kingdom**. Solomon found a good workman to assist him (7:13–14). Some might be surprised to find that Solomon makes use of Hiram, whose father was Phoenician, but Hiram had skill in metal work and that is what Solomon needed. The Christian

should not be afraid to use earthly knowledge and put it to spiritual use. *'All things are yours ... the world, life, death, the present, the future, all these things are yours'*. The Christian can use the common things of this world and put them to use for God's kingdom. Solomon was in control (*'he did all the bronze work **Solomon** wanted'*) and so Solomon was happy to have him work for God's temple.

2. **The architecture that was visible when you first approached the temple marked out two great principles of life**.

The temple had two large bronze pillars or columns at the front entrance of the temple (7:15). They had 'capitals' (decorations) at the top (7:16). Each column had bronze chains making a kind of symbolic basket (7:17) and inside the carving of a basket were carvings of pomegranates (a fruit about the size of an apple; 7:18).

The two columns did not hold anything; they were free-standing. Their significance was symbolic rather than practical. They had names, Jachin ('He Establishes') and Boaz ('In Him Is Strength'). They stood at the front of the building and attracted attention immediately as anyone approached it.

The two pillars stand for two basic principles in the kingdom of God. (i) 'He Establishes'. He is the one who says what His kingdom is. He has a plan for His people. (ii) 'In Him Is Strength'. If He is the one who has the right to say what His will is, He is also the one who gives the strength to see that His will is done.

The pomegranates were perhaps pictures of fruitfulness. It was as though there were baskets of fruit being held up at the tops of the two columns. When God's kingdom is done in His way ('He Establishes') and by His strength ('In Him Is Strength') baskets of fruitfulness will result, both the fruit of righteous character (as in Galatians 5:22–23) and the fruit of impact upon God's world (as in John 15:5).

The two columns were visible and prominent and stood at the front of the temple. They were two indications of what the kingdom of God was all about: God's work being established by God's strength. *'The LORD reigns'*, says the psalmist, *'The LORD is clothed with strength ... your throne is established'* (Psalm 93:1–2).

Chapter 11

The Place of Fellowship
(1 Kings 7:23–51)

Further details of the furnishings of the temple are now given to us. We learn of the 'sea' (7:23–26), the stands (7:27–37), the basins (7:38), how the stands and the sea were placed (7:39). Then we learn of the various utensils that were needed for the temple (7:40a). 1 Kings 7:40b–47 ends the sub-section with a list summarising the various metal works made by Hiram, and 1 Kings 7:48–51 ends the account of the building of the temple with a list of the treasures brought into it from the wealth of David and of Solomon.

1. **Before there can be access to the place of fellowship there must be atonement and cleansing.** So God provided a cleansing. **The sea** (7:23–26) was a gigantic bowl for the priests to wash in. It was called 'the sea' because it was so large. It was the equivalent of the laver in the tabernacle. There must be a cleansed conscience within and a cleansed life, before fellowship is possible. When the priest had washed himself in the 'sea', he was ready for access to God. The sea stood for cleansing in readiness for prayer, readiness for prayerful service of God. All God's people are 'priests'; they have access to Him. We must be clean priests to be able to effectively pray and to be used by God. 'The sea' represents for the Christian the vast power of the blood of Jesus to cleanse away our guilt and to cleanse our consciences.

The 'sea'.

It is clear that there were two courtyards around the temple. 2 Kings 23:12 refers to 'two courts'. There was an inner courtyard, mentioned in 6:36 and 7:12. This was used by the priests. Then there was yet another court around the area, which was for the people of Israel. When the Bible talks about the people going to the temple, it is to this area that it refers.

In the front of the inner court near the gate was the bronze altar, mentioned in 2 Chronicles 4:1. Further in was a 'molten sea'. These two objects were outside the actual building and were situated in the inner court, near the gate. Further in still, around the building were the **stands** (7:27–37) and **the basins** (7:38). They were down the side of the building (7:39) but were on wheels so they could be moved to the great altar when they were needed (see figure on p. 60).

The basins were there to wash the sacrifices and the utensils. Not only must the priests be washed, the sacrifices also had to be washed (see 2 Chronicles 4:6). The sacrifices were washed in the basins and then offered on the great altar. Jesus similarly was perfect in His life and then *'offered himself without blemish'* to God (Hebrews 9:14). It is only by

A stand carrying a basin.

the perfectly clean sacrifice of Jesus that one can begin to enter the place of fellowship. Then (moving further towards the building) after the priests were washed they were ready to enter the temple. All of this gives the Christian a way of interpreting the salvation of Jesus. The Christian enters the place of fellowship by means of the spotless sacrifice of Jesus for him, a sacrifice in which all his punishment for sin was carried by a Substitute. Then the Christian washes himself, cleanses his life from all sin, and he is ready for the place of fellowship and priestly ministry. There were smaller items also (7:40a), the **pots** to boil the meat of the peace offering, a sacrifice which symbolised peace with God and fellowship with His people, the **shovels** to clear away the ash and keep the fires burning, the **basins** to receive the blood of sacrifice. These have spiritual equivalents. Christ is our peace

(Ephesians 2:14); the fire of the Holy Spirit must be kept burning (Romans 12:20), the blood must be sprinkled on our consciences (Hebrews 9:14) to keep them clean.

2. **The place of fellowship is the place of peace and purity**. Just as there was to be no noise in the temple (6:7), similarly there was to be no dirt and grime in the temple. The preparation of all these materials was done in the plains of Jordan (7:40b–46), not within the temple itself which went up slowly and quietly, in peace and in purity.

3. **The place of fellowship is the place of faithful declaration of the wonders of God**. The gold stood for the glories of God. The nearer you were to the holy of holies, the more gold there was. Solomon left the bronze work and did not keep a record of how much bronze was used (7:47), but the gold materials he handled himself, no doubt with expert help (7:48). He wanted to see to it himself that the majesty and glory of God was represented by the presence of gold. He also brought in the gold that had been kept by David. He had not misused any of it, but had faithfully kept it to be used to express God's glorious presence (7:49–50).

Chapter 12

Honouring God

(1 Kings 8:1–21)

Now the temple has been built, but at the moment it does not have the ark of God. The ark was a wooden box, covered with gold, and with a gold lid. It expressed God's holiness; the law of Moses was kept within. And it expressed God's mercy; the blood of atoning sacrifice would be sprinkled on the gold cover. It was the place where God's glory would be shining out in the temple, and it was the point from which God would speak (see Joshua 7:6, 10). Everything in the temple has been built in the expectation that the ark will be in the holy of holies and the visible presence of God will come to be in Israel.

1. **Solomon honours God by confident faith**. Solomon knows that he is in the will of God. When the temple had been built, he assembled the leaders of the land at the time of the festival of tabernacles, and prepared to bring the ark from where it was being kept in a tent in Jerusalem (8:1–3a). He knows what will happen when the ark is installed in the temple, and waits eleven months (compare 6:38 with 8:2) for the time of the year when the biggest number of people come to Jerusalem. He moves with confidence. The priests carried the ark (8:3b), as was necessary, and the whole procession moved towards the new temple building (8:4). There were halts along the way and vast numbers of animals were sacrificed each time they stopped (8:5). Eventually the priests placed the ark in the holy of holies where the poles

for carrying it were left protruding out of the holy of holies so as to be visible from the holy place (8:6–8). This was a visible reminder that the ark was never to be touched. The ark was empty apart from the two stone tablets on which the ten commandments were written. In all this Solomon has a sure and certain knowledge that he is in God's will and is doing what God will honour. To know that what one is doing is in the will of God brings great faith; and great faith brings great blessing.

2. **God honoured Solomon by the coming down of His glory**. What would we think if after all of Solomon's seven years of building, God had not come down in glory as He had done in days gone by in the tabernacle? The confirmation that Solomon has been right to build the temple is that God honours him by coming down in obvious blessing. The cloud, the divine nature become partially visible, came down and filled the temple (8:10–11). This was the greatest proof there could be that Solomon's work was truly in God's will. God honoured everything that Solomon had done.

3. **God honoured Solomon despite his imperfections**. Solomon had great weaknesses. He had married pagan women (3:1). He had tolerated high places (3:3). There were aspects of his kingship which fell short of what he should have been as an Israelite king. The law of Moses had forbidden intermarriage with pagans (Deuteronomy 7:3), had forbidden the multiplication of horses, and had specially forbidden that trade in horses should lead to renewed contact with Egypt (Deuteronomy 17:16). The king was forbidden to take many wives (Deuteronomy 17:17), especially ones who would take him into idolatry. He was told not to accumulate gold or silver (Deuteronomy 17:18). Solomon was doing all of these things and it would eventually lead to his ruin. Yet what we have here is the proof that God can use His servants even when they are very far from being perfect. Solomon had made big mistakes in his life, but this did not prevent God from honouring him at this time. God does not always accuse, nor will He maintain His anger for ever. He does not treat us as our sins deserve or

repay us according to our iniquities (Psalm 103:9–10). Despite all his weaknesses Solomon had been seeking the honour of God in constructing the temple. So God honours him by coming down in the divine glory.

4. **Solomon honours God by faithfully instructing the people**. He recites a few lines which put into words what the temple was to be, a dwelling-place for the presence of God in Israel (8:12–13). But instruction of the people should be followed by intercession (as in John 14–16 followed by John 17, and Acts 20:17–35, followed by Acts 20:36). Solomon began to pray for the blessing of God upon the people (8:14). He looked back to the way in which God chose David and Jerusalem but had not allowed David to build the temple. Instead the privilege was reserved for Solomon (8:15–19). Now God's word had been fulfilled (8:20–21).

He blesses them by praying for them. It is a prayer full of thanksgiving. He recalls David's part in the project and recalls how God himself gave a revelation that Solomon should build the house.

Whatever weaknesses were in Solomon's life, and no matter what disaster they would later bring upon Solomon, at this point he was a fine and godly leader of God's people. He was honouring God, fulfilling what God had called him to do, and seeking to use the occasion to bless God's people. He was honouring God and so God honoured him. The greatest way God can honour us is to send down His presence upon what we are doing for Him. Whether that happens or not has much to do with the extent to which we seek Him and live for His presence to come down and be with us.

Chapter 13

Solomon's Prayer
(1 Kings 8:22–53)

Now we come to the details of Solomon's requests as he prays to God.

1. **Solomon set a wonderful example of leadership by his praying**. Here is a king standing before the altar, expecting to be heard because of the sacrifice made for his sin (8:22). He is in the presence of multitudes of the nation. He does not get the great high priest to pray. He was not shy to express his love for God and his need of God before tens of thousands of people, boldly spreading out his hands to God in prayer (8:22). At some point he knelt down (see 8:54) pleading for God to bless the nation. This is leadership. True leadership should never fear to confidently and publicly let it be known that our hope of blessing is in God and in God alone.

2. **As Solomon prays he is gripped with the knowledge of the faithful character of God**. He is overjoyed with the conviction that God is unique (*'There is no God like you'*) and faithful (*'who keeps covenant and mercy . . . '*, 8:23). He reviews the way in which God has been faithful thus far in the story of David's line. God's Word had been followed by God action. (*'You spoke with your mouth and you fulfilled it with you hand'*, 8:24).

3. **His great concern is that God will be with him and with his people**. He asks that the line of king David might be preserved. His prayer is building upon what God has said to

the house of David. Great praying is laying hold of what God has said. Solomon bases his petition on what he knows is the will and the promise of God. It gives us boldness and faith in prayer if we pray back to God the very things that He has promised (8:25–26). He asks that this very prayer he is praying might be received with favour (8:27–30). If it is to be so received God will have to overlook sins and weaknesses in Solomon's life. *'When you hear, forgive!'*

In Solomon's praying we see what it means to seek God. It is to be gripped with the conviction of God's greatness. It is to come to Him longing for His presence, and that He should fulfil our desire that we shall know Him and experience Him.

4. **Solomon looks for God's mercy in a great variety of circumstances**. He faces the future with great realism. His gaze stretches out into the future and he seems to envisage an abundance of painful circumstances that might face the nation of Israel. He prays for the people to be heard as they pray towards Jerusalem in a variety of circumstances (8:31–51). There will be disputes in the nation, where there is theft or fraud, and where dishonest people will swear falsely. Solomon prays for justice (8:31–32). There will be times of defeat as the result of sin (8:32–34) and times of drought (8:35–36), times of plague and famine (8:37–40) coming as the result of the people's sin. Solomon prays that God will forgive and restore them when they submit to the God who reveals Himself in His temple. The sacrifice of blood at the very gates makes it possible to pray and be accepted by God, despite a wicked past.

Solomon envisages that the revelation of God in Israel is not purely nationalistic; it reaches out to all peoples everywhere. The temple area is to be a house of prayer for all peoples (see Isaiah 56:6, 7). So he prays that people outside of Israel may come to know God through this temple (8:41–43). He knows, too, there will be times of battle (8:44–45) when they will need God's help (8:44–45).

Worst of all he knows the sin of the people could become so bad that God would uproot them from His land and send them into exile (8:46–51). Interestingly Solomon does not say they should pray towards the temple; he says they should pray *'towards their land'*. The situation could become so bad that the temple would be destroyed and only the land remain. This is in fact what happened four centuries later. In 586 BC the Babylonians destroyed the temple. Daniel in exile would pray towards the land of Israel (Daniel 6:10).

In all these varied circumstances that will face Israel in the future, Solomon asks that God will hear the people as they submit to this revelation of God in Jerusalem. The temple reveals God as a God of glory, a God who requires atonement by the shedding of blood, a God who can only be approached in a particular way. If the people will submit to such a God – a God who receives us when He is approached by the blood of a lamb – they will find mercy.

Solomon concludes this part of his prayer by asking that whenever the people cry out to God, in any situation, God will hear (8:52–53). It is no different for the modern Christian. All of the principles embodied in the temple are fulfilled in our Lord Jesus Christ. He is the great sacrifical Lamb by whom God is approached. He is the Great High Priest who offered the sacrifice. When His body was torn upon the cross, the veil of the temple was torn down by God. In Jerusalem, the way to God was opened up. When Jesus died upon the cross everything the temple pictured was fulfilled and the way into a 'holy of holies' level of fellowship was made open for all who believe, for all who confess their sin, for all who turn to the God of glory revealed in Jesus.

Chapter 14

The Praying King

(1 Kings 8:54–66)

Now Solomon gets up from his knees, turns around and faces the people, speaking before them with a loud voice (8:54–55). He now is partly thanking God, partly summarising in prayer all that he expects God to be doing for himself and the people.

1. **The continued blessing of God is a cause of great thanksgiving**. Although what he is doing is called 'blessing' the people (8:55) it still begins with thanksgiving towards God (8:56). He is grateful for blessings already bestowed. At a national level God has given the people rest (8:56) and has fulfilled everything that was being offered to Israel at the time of their first salvation. **Temple** is the fulfilment of **passover** (8:56). In Christian wording, **fellowship** is the fulfilment of **salvation**.

2. **The continued blessing of God is given in answer to God's appointed intercessor**. Solomon is like a king and a priest at the same time. His prayer is royal praying. He has been put in position over the people. He is there both to speak to God for the people and to speak to the people for God. His work is a foreshadowing of what Jesus, our great King and Priest constantly does for His people.

Solomon asks for God to give His presence. What Solomon prays for now is that this happy relationship between God and Israel should be maintained. *'The LORD be with us ... let Him not leave us ... '* (8:57).

Solomon asks for God to provide His grace (8:58). If God is with us He will incline our hearts to obedience. It is not just that obedience leads to God's being with us. Solomon's prayer takes it that God's being with us leads to obedience. It is not so much that obedience leads to grace (although that is true), but, more important, grace leads to obedience. Solomon is concerned that we should seek God's **grace**, God's **presence**. The temple is all about salvation by blood, salvation by mercy. One aproaches the temple as a sinner bringing the substitute, the sacrifice that is to die intead of the sinner. Failure in obedience results from failure in faith, failure in **seeking grace**. We come to **obedience** in no other way.

Solomon asks God to answer their prayer. He prays that God would remember these requests night and day (8:59), giving round-the-clock protection and nearness. Solomon represents Jesus, before Jesus came. Jesus similarly intercedes for His people day and night, ever living to make intercession in the heavenly temple, ever presenting the blood of His sacrifice.

Solomon asks God to enlarge His kingdom (8:60). The purpose of God blessing the people of Israel is that *'all the people of the earth may know that the* LORD *is God and that there is none other'*. Solomon wants Israel to be blessed that the world might be blessed.

3. **The continued blessing of God involves walking in obedience** (8:61). Although God will stay with Israel and will give His grace and enabling, each generation will need to persist in loyalty to Him, if they are to experience His blessings in their days. God will give grace; they must be willing to walk in obedience.

4. **The continued blessing of God involves the blessings symbolised in the temple** (8:62–66). Solomon dedicates the temple to God. Many sacrifices were presented to God. The burnt offerings speak of dedication, the meal offerings speak of consecration of one's work. Fellowship offerings speak of fellowship with God and with other people as a result of atonement for sin. It was a great day of enjoying fellowship

and companionship with God's people (8:62–63a). The house was consecrated (8:63b), the courts were dedicated (8:64a) and the great altar was insufficient to receive the vast quantities of what was brought for sacrifice.

For fourteen days people from the vast territory of Israel came for celebration. It was the feast of tabernacles. The people were commemorating their redemption and celebrating the building of the temple at the same time (8:65). They went home rejoicing (8:66).

The story of Solomon reaches its greatest height in this pinnacle of rejoicing and triumph. The glory of God was among His people. It was the thing that had been the purpose of their deliverance from Egypt. They were redeemed **from** something to be brought **to** something. They were taken from bondage to be brought to rest and the enjoyment of the glory of God in their midst.

But eventually the temple failed. Solomon's son would provoke the LORD (14:22) and Shishak would seize the treasures of God's house (14:25–26). Ahaz would commit ugly abominations (2 Kings 16:2–4) and would rob the house of God of more of its treasures (2 Kings 16:8), rebuilding parts of the temple following the designs of a pagan temple (2 Kings 16:8, 10–18). Manasseh would finally pollute the temple with immoral abominations (2 Kings 4–9). It would be destroyed by Nebuchadmezzar, rebuilt under Ezra and Nehemiah and further adorned by the Idumean king, Herod the Great. The priests and Sadducees would turn it into a den of robbers (Matthew 21:13). Jesus called it *'my Father's house'* (Luke 2:49) and the first disciples honoured it (Acts 2:46), but it was always only a piece of symbolism pointing forward to the temple of God in the person of Jesus, where God did indeed *'dwell on earth'* (1 Kings 8:27).

It was finally destroyed in AD 70. Never again will a central sanctuary have any great significance for God's people. Jesus is the great sacrifice for sin. His cross was the altar. Heaven is the mercy seat. Now the veil is taken down. All may enjoy the highest blessings of fellowship with God.

There will be no temple in heaven, because the whole heavens and earth will one day be one great 'holy of holies' for God's people to dwell with their Saviour. To Solomon was given the privilege of pointing to Jesus; the realities of these earthly bricks and stone come to pass through Jesus alone.

Chapter 15

Easy Life or Tough Journey?
(1 Kings 9:1–10:13)

Solomon had achieved everything he had desired to do (9:1). It was a dangerous state to be in. Now we discover the dangers facing Solomon and the blessings which are available to a pagan queen.

Consider, first, **the temptations coming upon Solomon**. When spiritual danger comes God often gives us warning. God appeared to Solomon to remind him of the conditions of blessing. It was the second time God had shown himself in this way (9:2). Now God accepted Solomon's prayer (9:3) and renewed an offer He had made before. Obedience would lead to the stability of the dynasty (9:4–5), said God (see 1 Kings 2:4, 3:14 and 6:12). Disobedience would lead to exile from the land, destruction of the temple and disgrace among the nations (9:6–9).

1. **Success can open the way to spiritual danger**. Solomon was coming into a comfortable and successful time of life. He has been king for twenty years and must have been at least in his forties at this time. He had spent twenty years in his two great building projects. He now was able to live in ease and luxury. Yet success is dangerous.

2. **Success came at the expense of a damaged relationship with a friend**. Hiram had given Solomon a lot of gold for his buildings. Apparently it could not be paid for by taxation and so Solomon gave some towns in payment for Hiram's gold. But Hiram was dissatisfied with what Solomon gave

him (9:10–14). Whether Hiram was pressing for unfair profit we cannot tell, but Solomon's success caused the loss of a friend.

3. **Success was gained at the expense of suffering for others**. The forced labour-gangs which Solomon had used for seven years to build the temple continued in existence **after** the temple was complete, and after the House of the Forest of Lebanon was built (another 13 years). The permanent forced labour was now doing damage to Solomon's kingdom and would eventually lead to disaster (9:15–23).

4. **A life of ease, fame, wealth and luxury was bringing Solomon nearer to a serious fall** (9:24–28; 10:1–13). He now was living a life of luxury. He added terraces to his wife's palace (9:24), and although he continued his life as a respectable law-abiding worshipper (9:25), he got involved in ship-building and international trade (9:26–28), and became famous throughout surrounding territories (10:1–13).

While Solomon was nearing disaster, the queen of Sheba was showing great eagerness to know about the God of Israel. Consider, secondly, **the great lengths to which the queen will go to find out about the name of the Lord**. She heard about *'the reputation of Solomon in relation to the name of the LORD'* (10:1). Solomon's earthly achievements aroused the regard of a fellow ruler, but it was the possibility that Solomon's success came through the LORD that interested her. The news had got to Arabia (where the land of Sheba was to be found) that there was a great and mighty king in Israel whose greatness had something to do with *'the name of the Lord'* and who had a built a house simply to be a place where Israel's God would place His name.

1. **She went to great lengths to find out about God**. 'Sheba' was the home of the Sabeans in south-west Arabia, in what is today called Yemen. She travelled about 1200 miles, presumably by camel, to find out about someone who had been blessed through the name of the Lord.

2. **She came with great eagerness** (10:2). Not every pagan king or queen of the ancient world responded in this way. Most kings and queens of the ancient world responded with hatred to the claims of Israel. But God can work in anyone's heart and the queen of Sheba had been drawn to Israel.

3. **She came with many questions**. These were not riddles or intellectual puzzles. More likely they were questions about 'the name of the LORD' and how to be a successful ruler.

This is the way people baffled by the perplexities of life may come to Jesus, who is *'greater than Solomon'* (Matthew 12:42). We come determinedly, eagerly, bringing the troubles that burden and baffle us.

4. **She made some satisfying discoveries**. The queen found that Solomon knew a great deal about all sorts of things (10:3). She discovered his **wisdom** (10:3, 4a), his **palace** (10:4b), the goodness of his **food** (10:5), the privileges of his servants who were standing and his servants who were sitting. She appreciated the advantages of his cupbearers, the wonders of his offerings (10:5) and the amazing character of his wisdom (10:6).

If we explore the unsearchable riches of Christ, we shall discover the vastness of His wisdom, His treasures of knowledge, His food for eternal life, the privileges of being seated in the heavenly places, the privileges of standing in grace and in readiness to do His will.

5. **She came to know these things by personal experience**. At first she must say *'I heard ... but I did not believe...'* (10:6–7) but later she has come to experience God's blessings for herself and discovers *'not even half was told me'*. (10:8). She comes to faith in the God of Israel. She believes in His choice of Israel, His choice of Solomon, His being the God of righteousness and justice (10:9). In the visit of the queen of Sheba we see how Jesus is worthy of honour from the nations of the world. We see her eagerly become a friend of God's king, Solomon (10:10). The report goes on to tell how Solomon brought gold (10:11) and valuable

wood (10:12) and used it for the king's house. The queen now had a generous and powerful friend in Solomon (10:13).

Solomon himself was slipping into complacency, but in contrast here is one who will travel a thousand miles and more to find the truth about God's name from one of God's servants. Whose position are we in, Solomon's or that of the queen of Sheba?

Chapter 16

Solomon's Fall

(1 Kings 10:14–11:8)

Solomon was coming into a level of glory that was too great for any mortal to bear. The degree of admiration Solomon was getting was appropriate to Jesus alone. There is no one who is *'worthy to receive power and riches and wisdom and might and honour and glory and blessing'* except the Lamb of God (Revelation 5:12). Two main guidelines emerge from his story.

1. **Worldly glory has a tendency towards spiritual ruin**. Solomon's greatness prepared the way for spiritual decline. The description of the queen of Sheba's visit shows how great and famous Solomon had become. He became unbelievably wealthy (10:14–17). He had initially acquired gold for adorning the temple. But what had once been done for God was now being done for Solomon. Yet the law forbade the accumulation of gold by the king (Deuteronomy 17:18). His gold shields (10:17) had no function except to express his boastfulness. He built a grandiose throne (10:18–20) and even his household utensils were needlessly luxurious (10:21). Did he really need to drink out of gold drinking cups? He was now using his wealth and his power for selfish purposes (10:22). At one time Solomon had poured his effort into building a place for the glory of God's name; now he is pouring his efforts into collecting apes and peacocks! He was given great fame and honour (10:23–5). He was richer, 'wiser', more sought-after than any king of

that day (10:24–25) and year by year was growing wealthier (10:26–29. He collected vast quantities of horses and chariots (10:26–29).

But few people come into such a high level of success without being corrupted by prosperity. Most people need some adversity from time to time. A person who never suffers, never struggles, never is despised by anyone, is likely to become corrupt. It is hard for the rich to experience the kingdom of God.

The multiplication of horses, and the accumulation of gold were specifically denounced by the Mosaic regulations concerning kingship. How can Solomon feel that he is somehow exempt from the commands of God concerning the king?

2. **One piece of rebelliousness against God can ruin our lives and our ministry**. Solomon's failure came because of pagan women. *'Now the king, Solomon, loved many foreign women...'* (11:1). The law had forbidden it (11:2). *'You shall not intermarry with them'*, said Moses (Deuteronomy 7:3). Even before he became king, Solomon was careless about marrying outside of Israel's covenant faith. Solomon first married Naamah, a Moabitess (see 14:21). Then when he became king he took another pagan wife, Pharaoh's daughter. Then he made more alliances, and then even more, all of them with important women from surrounding nations. Eventually he had a vast number of alliances with pagan women (11:3). There was nothing wrong with marrying a foreigner, so long as she shared the faith of Israel. It was not because they were interracial or inter-tribal that Solomon's marriages were wrong; they were wrong because they were inter-faith!

Solomon began to sympathize with pagan religions. As he became elderly his heart was not devoted to the LORD (11:4), then he actually began to indulge in the worship of false gods (11:5–6). David would have been horrified.

Solomon had a gift for friendship. We have seen how well he related (most of the time) to Hiram, and how he secured a good friendship with the queen of Sheba. It seems that he could relate rather well to the kings and rulers of the surrounding nations. The way of cementing a friendship in the international politics of the ancient world was to take into one's home or palace the daughter of the friendly ruler. For the country who provided the bride, it was a way of having an ambassador in the country of the son-in-law. For the country whose king married the daughter it gave a kind of guarantee against military invasion. No neighbouring king would be likely to invade the country of his daughter and son-in-law. Solomon seemed to feel that he could follow these practices of ancient kingship.

But it was fatal. To be friendly to the extent of marrying the neighbouring king's daughter meant that one was being friendly also to the religion of the neighbouring king. The royal wife would want Solomon to show tolerance to her idolatrous faith. The whole business was a way for pagan religions to grow increasingly acceptable in Israel. This is what happened. Centuries later Nehemiah said *'There was no king like Solomon who was loved by God, yet foreign women made even him to sin'* (Nehemiah 13:26).

Close friendships have a lot of impact upon us for good or evil. When we are close to godly people we are likely to learn from them. When we are closely bound with wicked people we are likely to pick up wicked ways ourselves. The closeness of Solomon's relationship with these foreign princesses and nobles was that he grew cold toward the Lord, grew less zealous for the purity of worship in Israel. David's sin with Bathsheba no doubt damaged the kingdom, but this was something vastly more serious. Solomon was even building places of worship for the false gods (11:7, 8)

The man who is famous for wisdom came to great foolishness. He ruined his country, and even his glorious temple was eventually destroyed because of the idolatry he himself had introduced. The wisest man in the history of the world was also the biggest fool in the history of the world. He made foolish friendships with pagan people, he disregarded the written Scriptures, he inwardly turned away from God and showed amazing perversity in himself practising idolatry.

Chapter 17

Reaping the Whirlwind

(1 Kings 11:9–39)

Solomon's lapse into idolatry brought terrible calamities into his life.

1. **Sin angers God** (11:9–10). God had been patient with Solomon for a long time. He had not punished him when he married Pharaoh's daughter (3:1). It was as if God was saying 'Let us see. Maybe he will resist the temptations to worship her gods'. God did nothing when Solomon tolerated the high places of pagan worship (3:2). While Solomon's heart was sincere God tolerated a lot of blemishes (3:3). God gave him the amazing offer of anything he wanted to ask for (3:5), gave him great success and great wealth (see 4:20–21, 29–30), gave him the high privilege of building the temple, heard his prayer at the dedication of the temple and sent His glory down to honour all that Solomon had done. Then God had appeared to Solomon a second time to give him explicit warning about the consequences of idolatry. Did Solomon not think the warning of 1 Kings 9:6 was seriously intended? Apparently he felt that he had fulfilled his life's ambitions. He felt he was now elderly and thought God's threat need not worry him.

But it was a serious matter to turn to sin in old age. God became angry. Solomon ruined his relationship with God. John the apostle wrote *'Watch yourselves, that you might not lose what you have accomplished, but that you may receive a full reward'* (2 John 8).

81

2. **Sin may deprive us of the blessing of God**. God had been patient and tolerant with Solomon but now he was deprived of his greatest blessings (11:11–13). His line would suffer the loss of the bulk of the nation of Israel. It had taken David time and effort before he was able to become king of all Israel. For a long time ten northern tribes had stayed independent. Only after seven years did David become the ruler of the entire kingdom, and it was over the entire nation that Solomon became king when David died. But now his line will lose the bulk of the kingdom. Northern Israel will withdraw from the rule of the Davidic line. Solomon's descendants would rule only Judah and the associated tribe of Benjamin.

3. **Sin may be punished by the raising up of external enemies** (11:14–25). Solomon had been known for his peace. Unlike David he had never been a soldier. For many years he had ruled without any external enemies. Now, as a result of his sin, God raises up enemies against him. There was an Edomite who held a grudge against Solomon. His father had been murdered by Joab, David's military commander, so he had reason to hate David's son. David had died twenty years previously and Hadad had not felt it necessary to get vengeance. But God's displeasure towards Solomon showed itself in God's raising up an enemy to distress Solomon.

Another enemy was Rezon who also had cause to hate David's son (11:23–25). He was ruler in Damascus, capital of the nearby kingdom of Aram or Syria. So Solomon had two enemies who were near at hand to harass him. Edom was not far to the south and Syria was not far to the north. The two could combine to menace Solomon. The 'prince of peace' lost his peace because of his departing from his obedience to the LORD.

4. **Sin may be punished by the raising up of an internal enemy** (11:26–39). God had until this point protected Solomon but now that Solomon had departed from God, God was removing the protection. So not only were there external enemies, a foe from within his own people arose also. When God wishes to chasten us for our sinful ways his

protection can easily be lifted. Despite a lifetime of peace Solomon finds himself in the midst of disturbing conflicts.

Jeroboam also becomes an enemy to Solomon (11:26). Solomon had been impressed with him during one of his building projects (11:27–28). At such a time Jeroboam had seen an oppressive side to Solomon's kingdom. We have seen before in Solomon's story how his use of forced labour went on too long and was rousing resentment within the nation. Jeroboam had firsthand experience of a cause of discontent within Solomon's rule. At such a time a prophet came to Jeroboam with a message that he was being called to be the leader of secession within the country (11:29–32). The reason why Solomon should lose part of the kingdom was explicitly given to Jeroboam. The rupture was God's response to idolatry in Solomon (11:33). Jeroboam is told both the extent of what would be given to Jeroboam and the timing of its being given to him (11:34–37). Jeroboam had already been wanting to take the northern tribes and God was giving him 'all that your soul desires' (11:37). Solomon has yet another enemy.

As these things were happening to Solomon he could have turned to God in humility and repentance. Actually Solomon did nothing. God announced judgement but Solomon seems to have made no attempts to repent or ward off the judgement of God. He could have cast himself on the mercy of God. He could have thanked God that God had warned him. When God announces judgement the reason why He speaks is that we might repent and avert the judgement. Solomon could have pleaded for forgiveness. Hezekiah was able to turn aside God's judgement. Manasseh found forgiveness. Ahab found forgiveness. Solomon could have found forgiveness also. He could have torn down the idols of his wives and pleaded for mercy. But he did not. The wisest king became the biggest fool.

Chapter 18

Solomon's End
(1 Kings 11:37–43)

There is no reason to think that Jeroboam was at first a greatly wicked person. Later on he *'made Israel to sin'* but in his early days he may have been quite sincere. He was concerned with Solomon's oppression, and wanted to do something about it. He is given what he wants (*'all that you desire'*, 11:37). God offers him a family line of rulers just as the line of king David was to rule in Judea (11:38–39). If Jeroboam had taken God seriously a line of kings would have lasted for many years in northern Israel, all of them descendants of Jeroboam. He could have been famous for righteousness instead of (as actually happened) becoming famous for sin. At this point God is doing to Solomon what he did to Saul, taking the kingdom from him and giving it to a near neighbour. Only small Judea would stay with the house of David.

Here the story is being told to us as part of what was happening to Solomon. God chastised Solomon by raising up a rival near at hand. It is all part of God's chastening Solomon for the sin of idolatry. When a believer sins there may come strange adversities and enmities from all around. God seems to treat us as an enemy and on all sides he blocks the way to blessing. The consequences of sin continue.

5. **Sin brings about defeat and personal frustration** (11:40). Solomon knew about the prophecy, apparently, and did his best to kill Jeroboam but God overruled and Solomon

experienced personal frustration in what he was seeking to do (11:40). Saul had tried to kill David but failed; Solomon was trying to kill Jeroboam but failed. Sin brings upon us a strange blindness. Did Solomon think he could overthrow a prediction from a prophet of God? He evidently believed the prophecy that was given to Jeroboam because he was trying to overthrow it by murdering his successor. But *'the counsel of the Lord shall stand'*. Solomon cannot overthrow God's Word. His foolishness is all part of the blindness that comes upon us when we are out of God's will. But the result is only personal frustration and failure. When God has decided to chasten us no amount of struggling and manipulation can overthrow God's decision.

6. **Sin may bring about final shame and stain**. Solomon ruined his life. He died in his sins (11:41–43). He lost his reward. He was saved through *'fire'* (1 Corinthians 3:15).

Solomon *threw away many advantages*. He had come to know the Lord when he was young. He had been given discernment and earthly greatness. He had riches and fame, vision and skill. He could have used his eminence for God, but he threw it all away because of his foolish preoccupation with cultivating political alliances with surrounding paganism.

Solomon *resisted warnings*. God warned him in a very forthright way, speaking to him directly about the continuation of his royal line. Idolatry would destroy his future descendants, God said. Then chastenings came upon him but still Solomon took no notice. When enemies were raising themselves against him he could have asked why God was allowing it. When a man's ways please the LORD, He makes even his enemies to be at peace with him (Proverbs 16:7). When a man's ways do not please the LORD, he may find enemies being raised up against him.

Solomon *felt the written Scripture could be disregarded*. Deuteronomy chapter 17 had laid down the rules concerning kingship. Solomon somehow felt that he did not have to apply the Scripture to himself. Despite written warnings against gold, horses and women, Solomon spent much of his

life with gold, horses and pagan idolatrous women. So
Solomon's life ended in shame. David's closing days ended in
great ascriptions of praise to God (2 Chronicles 28, 29).
Solomon's story ends abruptly. He was an Old Testament
example of the principle of 1 Corinthians 3:15. There is to
be a judgement of the saved, and there is the possibility of
some of the saved doing badly in the day of God's judgement. There is no reason to believe that Solomon went to
eternal punishment, but he certainly ruined his life and lost
his reward for faithfulness.

If Solomon had repented he would have escaped loss at
the judgement seat. *'If we would judge ourselves we would not
be judged'*, said Paul (1 Corinthians 11:31), but Solomon did
not judge himself even when the most clear warnings were
being given to him by the Lord. There is such a thing as a
believer 'suffering loss' at the judgement seat of Christ.
Solomon is an Old Testament example of someone who did
not endure to the end in his godliness and will undoubtedly
'suffer loss' in the day of judgement. Despite Solomon's
preoccupation with gold he ended his life in what Paul
would call a building of wood, hay and stubble.

So the great Solomon was a flawed character. Where can
there be found a king to follow David? We shall see one king
after another in 1 Kings, but they are all flawed characters,
some more than others. Even the 'good' kings, like
Solomon, end up making some great mistake or ruining
their testimony. None of them gets to the end of their story
with a flawless record. The truth is only Jesus is worthy to be
the 'Son of David'. He has the greatness of the best kings, *'in
all points but without sin'*. If we are to reign with Christ we
must be close to our king. Otherwise we might be more like
Solomon than like Jesus.

Chapter 19

Learning From Prophecy
(1 Kings 12:1–24)

After the reign of Solomon the land of Israel divided into two countries. 'Israel' now will mean northern Israel, consisting of ten tribes. 'Judah' is the southern tribal territory. The story in 1 Kings 12:1–24 gives us a picture of how God gets His will done in the affairs of the nations.

1. **God can give prophetic pointers to the future**. We recall that God had given a word to Solomon concerning the division of the kingdom (see 11:11–13). What is happening here is that the word of prophecy is being fulfilled. God rules easily among the nations. In the midst of human planning and human turmoil, God is at work. He knows His will, He announces His will to His servants the prophets, and He can bring about His will with no difficulty.

It was a major tragedy that the kingdom had to divide into two. It weakened what was an influential empire, losing all the power that David and Solomon had built up. It was God's judgement upon the nation's idolatry. Much that is gained by worship of the LORD will be lost if other gods are revered.

2. **God can hand a man over to error in order to bring about His own will**. Rehoboam, Solomon's son and his successor on the throne, begins with high hopes. He has confidence that the kingdom will come to him; almost everyone is supporting him. All Israel goes to Shechem (12:1), a

northern city, to make him king. It seems that the northerners were willing to have Rehoboam as their king but they
wanted their own cultural identity to be respected, and an
injustice corrected.

However rulers rule by the grace of God. At any moment
the LORD can hand a leader over to the consequences of his
own folly. Kingdoms can be taken away from their rulers
with great ease. Despite Rehoboam's great advantages
God has said that the kingdom will be divided and God is
about to fulfil His word. So various events come together
to rob Rehoboam of much of his kingdom and bring about
the fulfilment of what God had predicted.

Jeroboam came back (12:2)! A delegation from northern
Israel ask for the policy of forced labour to be made easier
(12:3–4). At this point God allowed Rehoboam to make a
mistake. He asks for time to consider (12:5) but listens to the
wrong people (12:6–11) and makes a bad mistake. A harsh
answer is given (12:12–14). It is a blunder to think that
harshness and severity is the right way to lead a people.
Solomon had been foolishly inclined to severity and had an
arrogant attitude towards his own authority. It is part of the
ignorance of youth to think that severity and harshness will
bring about loving obedience! Experience teaches otherwise.
The older one gets, the more one realises the need for gentleness. We all need to listen to others. Job speaks words of
wisdom when he says he has not *rejected the cause of my
manservant or my maidservant when they brought a
complaint against me'* (Job 31:13). Gentleness will do what
violence cannot do. Kindly words would have been easy for
Rehoboam. The whole kingdom was ready to follow him
and a few words of encouragement would have satisfied
them. The days of Solomon had been days of prosperity.
But God let Rehoboam fall into foolishness. It all came
from God. It was a *'turn of affairs brought about by the
LORD'* (12:15). God finds it so easy to bring about His will.
He can hand men and women over to their own foolishness
any time He pleases. He is **able** to keep us from falling but
He does not have to do so!

3. **When God acts He can act powerfully**. Sometimes we can sense God is working things together even in events that we think ought not to have happened. The people sing a traditional song which rallies the northerners to withdrawal (12:16). It had been sung before (see 2 Samuel 20:1) in days when Sheba had tried to take the northern tribes away from David. Now the northern Israelites returned home regarding themselves as an independent nation (12:16). Rehoboam has only Judah and Benjamin left to him plus some northern Israelites living in Judean towns (12:17).

Rehoboam is slow to see that God's word is indeed about to be accomplished. When God acts in history according to His will nothing can turn back what He wants to do. Rehoboam thinks he can continue as before and sends to the workers Adoram, the manager of the forced labour-gangs. But he soon learns that things have now changed. The goodwill he had has been lost. Adoram is killed. The days of forced labour are finished and Rehoboam himself narrowly escapes with his life (12:18). The division between Israel and Judah becomes permanent (12:19) and Jeroboam becomes king of northern Israel (12:20).

4. **Suffering is lessened if the prophetic word is heeded**. Rehoboam was ready to go to war to bring the northern territories back into submission (12:21) but a prophetic message persuaded them to abandon the idea. The division of the kingdom was from the Lord (12:22–24). If Solomon had heeded God's word (11:11–13) the division might have been delayed or might not have happened. If Rehoboam had heeded the same revelation Adoram would not have been killed. He himself would not have almost lost his life. Rehoboam is unbelieving and slow to learn that God's words through His prophets are trustworthy and must be heeded. Eventually he heeds a prophetic message and war is prevented. Suffering is lessened if the prophetic word is heeded but some are slow to learn.

Chapter 20

False Religion

(1 Kings 12:25–33)

Jeroboam is the fourth king in the story of Israel, and the third whose story is told in the book of Kings. In 1 Kings **Saul** has been ignored; **David** did right in everything except in the matter of Uriah the Hittite (15:5); **Solomon** walked in the ways of David but tolerated high places (3:3) and fell into idolatry (11:33).

Jeroboam (931–910 BC) introduced an idolatry that ruined the life of Israel for two centuries and then destroyed it. Twenty-three times in the book of Kings we shall be told that Jeroboam made Israel sin (1 Kings 14:16; 15:26, 30, 34; 16:2, 19, 26, 31; 21:33; 22:52; 2 Kings 3:3; 10:29, 31; 13:2, 6; 14:24; 15:9, 18, 24, 28; 17:21, 22; 23:15).

We see, first, **the great wickedness of idolatry**. A major theme of 1 and 2 Kings is the destructiveness of idolatry. Blessing and cursing came upon the nation of Israel according to whether or not they were loyal to God as the one and only God.

'Idolatry' is often not taken seriously. Sometimes it is said, 'It does not matter what religion you have; all religions believe in the same God'. However Islam and Hinduism and faith in the Lord Jesus Christ are all very different things, and if one is true the others are not. What will determine whether God is truly blessing anyone's life or whether God is blessing a country is whether the only God and Father of our Lord Jesus Christ is acknowledged. Failure to acknowledge the God of the Bible is idolatry.

Jeroboam chose Shechem as his capital and made a fortress out of Peniel (12:25). Apparently he wanted to protect himself from all possible invasions. Also he felt threatened by the nearby kingdom of Judah (12:26, 27) and thought that his life was in danger (12:28). So he made two calves and proclaimed them as gods. They were typical of pagan religions. Egypt had gods who were represented by a bull. When the Israelites had first left Egypt they tried to represent God by a golden calf (Exodus 32:1–6), but the nation had aroused God's anger at that time. Now Jeroboam is doing the same thing again. Bethel and Dan became centres of the new religion (12:29–30).

Jeroboam also set up 'high places', open-air places of worship. He made non-Levitical priests, who did not descend from the tribe of Levi as was required by God's law (12:31). He made a new festival, altering the festivals that God required in the Mosaic law (12:32–33).

Secondly, we consider **what led him into idolatry**. It was not a matter of his convictions about religion; it was certainly not because God had revealed the truth to him. Jeroboam's religion was man-made. *'After giving thought to the matter'* (as 12:28 should be translated), Jeroboam introduced a perverse religion of his own imagining into Israel. It was a step towards polytheism. His gods were not bothered about purity of life. Immorality and wickedness came into the life of the nation. Rejecting a God of glory led Jeroboam into supporting a religion of perversity. The human race is powerfully religious. Take away the true God and men and women will soon find a perverse deity to fill the gap.

A 'god' is something which we think is supremely valuable and to which we look for refuge in every time of need. An 'idol' is any other 'god' than the God who revealed Himself through Israel, the God and Father of our Lord Jesus Christ. There is crude idolatry, the worship of statues and images of various kinds. And there is subtle idolatry, the worship of money and property. The person who has money regards it as supremely valuable, the thing to which he will fly for refuge in time of need. The modern idol is often material wealth or sucess among one's friends. But it is an idol, a 'new religion'. Like Jeroboam's new religion it involves a refusal to build one's life on God's promises. Jeroboam had at first been concerned about Solomon's oppression, and wanted to do something about it. In the early stage of his life, God offered him a kingship that would be passed on from generation to generation in his family. He would be the beginning of a line of rulers (11:38–39). But the offer was conditional. God said *'If you ... walk in my ways ... keeping my statutes ... I will build you an enduring house'* (11:38). But Jeroboam is not living in the faith that God's promise is reliable. He acted on what was said to him about being king, but he does not act on what was said to him about obedience to the one and only LORD.

He was using religion for political purposes. There is no reason to think that Jeroboam had the slightest interest in the truth or the falsity of these gods of his. He did not really believe that the two idols of Bethel and Dan were truly deities who had brought about the deliverance from Egypt. It was simply that some kind of religion was needed otherwise the people might be loyal to Judah in the south. Jeroboam had an entirely man-made religion. He simply invented a religion that was politically supportive of his position as king of northern Israel. The question whether there was any truth in all that he was doing did not seem to bother him at all.

Of course it was doomed. All our idolatries are destined to collapse. The consequences of idolatry may take many years to work out but any people who favour any god other than the God and Father of our Lord Jesus Christ are inviting disaster into their lives

Chapter 21

A Tale of Two Prophets

(1 Kings 13:1–32)

Jeroboam adopted a false religion for purely secular reasons. He was more concerned about his own advantage than about the truth of God. Yet God gave him warnings and opportunities to turn around. There came a time when he received a striking word from God that ought to have made him pull back from the direction he was taking. It is a striking example of how predictive prophecy works, and we can learn from it something of how prophecy works in every age.

1. **When a true prophet makes predictions he is precise and definite and able to be checked eventually**. A prophet comes from Judah and comes to Jeroboam's newly-made altar in Bethel, at a time when the king is offering incense (one remembers that only priests were to offer incense). He gives a very specific and clear prediction. One day a Judean king will come, Josiah by name, who will destroy the idolatry that Jeroboam is promoting (13:1–2). It was a very specific prophecy. One day it would be able to be checked. This is how true prediction in Scripture works. One thinks of Jesus' predictions concerning Jerusalem (Matthew 24:2) and Isaiah's prediction concerning Cyrus (Isaiah 45:1). Within 1 Kings one thinks of Elijah's prediction concerning rain (17:1).

2. **Prophecy may be accompanied by signs**. This unidentified man of God predicted that Jeroboam's altar would split

apart (13:3). If it happened without manipulation it would be clear evidence of the miraculous.

3. **True prophets are fearless people**. This man of God was clearly in danger from Jeroboam (13:4). The true prophet gets a lot of persecution but it does not prevent him from speaking what he is given. Jeroboam orders the man's arrest but immediately his hand is paralysed in a stretched out position (13:4). The true prophet gets a lot of opposition but he gets a lot of protection also! Jeroboam encounters a rebuke from God (13:4); the altar dramatically splits apart (13:5) and it takes the intercession of the prophet before Jeroboam is restored (13:6). The prophet may get heavenly vindication. It makes him confident and fearless.

4. **The true prophet gets a lot of special guidance**. The king invites this man home and offers him a reward (13:7), but the prophet says 'no' (13:8). He has been given special instructions from the Lord (13:9) which he obeys (13:10).

5. **True prophecy may be imitated**. Having been used by God, the prophet proceeds to go home. But there is a retired prophet in the area of Bethel who wants to spend time with the prophet from Judah. So he goes after the Judean prophet (13:11–14) and asks him to visit the second prophet's home in Bethel (13:15). At first the man from Judea declines (13:16–17) but at this point the prophet of Bethel gives a fake prophecy of his own. This man has been given prophecies in the past and knows how to act like a prophet. He brings a counterfeit 'word from the Lord' (13:18). It is very convincing, and carelessly the prophet of Judah does not test the prophecy from the man of Bethel and so is led into making a serious mistake. This shows us that prophecy can be counterfeited. Prophecies need to be tested. The prophet from Judah is led into disobedience and goes back to the home of the prophet of Bethel (13:19).

6. **True prophecy does not prove anyone's spirituality**. Suddenly God comes upon the older, backslidden, retired, prophet and he is given a word from God for the prophet of Judea (13:20–23). When the Judean prophet goes on his way, he is killed by a lion (13:24). The news gets back to

Bethel (13:25–26) and the older prophet takes care of the burial (13:27–29). He grieves for the younger man (13:30) and wants one day to be buried with him (13:31). He knows the younger man was an authentic prophet and that his word will be fulfilled (13:32). It shows that prophecy can be given to anyone anywhere.

We still need prophecy today. I do not mean by this that we need new revelations or new doctrines. I mean that we need to stay in touch with the living God, and other Christians may be given words from the Lord to help us. The greatest form of prophecy is powerful preaching where the preacher is having words virtually put into his mouth as he preaches in the Holy Spirit. But there are lesser forms of prophecy, which is why we are told not to despise them (1 Thessalonians 5:20).

Yet the matter needs to be handled with care. Predictions need to be precise and a person whose predictions do not turn out right is to be viewed with suspicion. Anything that claims to be miraculous is of little value if it is manipulated. A 'prophet' is a person who is frequently used in the gift of prophecy. There do not seem to be many of them around, but we need to stay open to people who are used in this way. However everything needs to be tested and prophecy may be imitated. Even one who has been truly used may at any one point be making a mistake. The gift of prophecy – or any other dramatic gift – does not prove the person concerned is always right or always spiritual.

The Judean prophet was dealt with more severely than the older backslidden prophet. Yet one can see the reason for this. The nation of Israel would have heard about the Judean prophet's prophey concerning the future ministry of Josiah. The Lord's judgement on the Judean prophet for disobedience made it clear that the whole matter was authentically from God. The greater the privilege in serving God, the greater is our accountability.

Chapter 22

Jeroboam

(1 Kings 13:33–14:20)

The prophecy that Jeroboam received from the Judean prophet had little impact upon him. He continues to promote his idolatry. 1 Kings notes that it is this very idolatry that will cause the extermination of the royal line of Jeroboam (13:33–34).

1. **Miraculous prophecy can be used to call us to godliness.** Jeroboam is a case of a person who believes in the supernatural but has no interest in submitting to God. Miracles attract our attention but they do not compel saving faith. Earlier in his life Jeroboam had received a dramatic prediction from a prophet called Abijah (11:29–38). He had been pleased when Abijah predicted Jeroboam's kingship. Abijah's prediction confirmed him in his desire to be a rival to Rehoboam and to take over the kingdom after Solomon died. However the same prediction that encouraged Jeroboam to take the northern kingdom also warned him to walk in the ways of the law of God. Solomon's son lost most of the kingdom because of Solomon's idolatry (11:33). Jeroboam will retain his kingdom – said Abijah – if he stays away from idolatry (11:38). Jeroboam has been happy with the prediction about taking over Solomon's kingdom but has taken no notice about the part of Abijah's words that urged him to keep God's law. He had not responded in faith to the call to walk in the ways of God.

Now Jeroboam wants the miraculous again! This time he wants to hear that his son will recover, but he does not want personally to submit his life to God. Jeroboam's son becomes ill (14:1). Ahijah had given him a prediction before, so Jeroboam decides to consult him again but he does not want to face a word from God about his own sins. So he suggests his wife should go instead of him, and she must go in disguise (14:2). She must give a gift (14:3) and Ahijah will give her a message.

Jeroboam expects Ahijah to have supernatural knowledge and yet believes Ahijah will be deceived by a disguise. It does not seem to occur to him that if God can reveal the future, He can reveal the present!

2. **God wants us to submit to Him in areas of weakness or sinfulness**. Jeroboam's belief that Ahijah can give miraculous predictions is of no value to Jeroboam because he has refused to respond in faith to God's demand that he keep free from idolatry. Jeroboam wants only to manipulate the supernatural.

Jeroboam receives a very severe rebuke. Belief in the miraculous will not prevent sin from being judged. The disguise is useless. Ahijah is elderly and almost blind but God still speaks to him (14:4–5a). Ahijah is told what to say (14:5b) and welcomes Jeroboam's wife as she comes through the door.

The disguise is futile (14:6). Ahijah has a message. Jeroboam had not responded to God's offer of a long-lasting family line of kings (14:7–8). He has been as much an idolater as Solomon whose kingdom was shattered because of idolatry (14:9). His family-line of kings will be *'cut off'*. The little boy *'who urinates against the wall'* (as the Hebrew should be literally translated), that is *'every last male'*, will be abandoned and disgraced (14:10), and will be without any honourable burial (14:11). Jeroboam has refused to submit to God in an area of sinfulness in his life.

3. **God gives us many hints that He wants our submission**. Jerboam had experienced things that were enough to make him know that God was real. The supernatural knowledge

that enabled the nearly blind Ahijah ought again to convince Jeroboam and his wife that God is real. Also he apparently had one godly son whose testimony ought to have led him to repentance. The very reason why Jeroboam's son is being taken to God is that he is a godly child. As Jeroboam's wife goes back the boy will die (14:12). He is *'the only one in the family of Jeroboam in whom the* LORD, *the God of Israel, has found anything good'* (14:13). Apparently Jeroboam's son had been kept by God in the ways of godliness. Jeroboam had someone within his own family who was a witness of what God could do.

God will allow someone to arise who will bring the family line of kings to an end (14:14; its fulfilment is recorded in 1 Kings 15:25–30). Eventually northern Israel will be removed from the territory altogether (14:15–16). The proof that this is a word from God is that it will begin to come true as soon as Jeroboam's wife enters the city. This is exactly what happens (14:17–18). But it still does not lead Jeroboam to repentance. The many things he did are mentioned by 1 Kings (14:19) but they are not of eternal significance and they are not told in detail. Jeroboam died; his son Nadab succeeded him (14:20) but Nadab was not destined to rule long. The word of God would soon be fulfilled (see 15:25–30).

Are you a person who 'uses' religion? Some people have a belief in the reality of miraculous prophecy and yet will not submit to God. God had offered Jeroboam a successful future, but he would not accept God's offer. Do you make that mistake? There are people who can be highly 'religious' and have what seems to be a faith in the miraculous. Yet they only want the miraculous for their own purposes. Somehow they miss the godly and purposeful life that God is offering them. They gain the miraculous predictions but they lose their souls. Let us not be one of them. God's words to us must lead us to faith in His Saviour. God speaks to us in order to save us.

Chapter 23

Rehoboam, Abijam, Asa
(1 Kings 14:21–15:24)

The question now is: how will the kings of the two separate kingdoms move forward? The northern kingdom went badly from its earliest days. How will the southern kingdom get along? Is there any possibility that there will come a king who will be able to turn the nation back to God? The next three rulers of Judah failed. Rehoboam **furthered** idolatry. Abijam **tolerated** idolatry. Asa **resisted** idolatry but damaged his usefulness to God in later years.

1. **The lesson of Rehoboam's reign is: unless God intervenes idolatry brings increasing spiritual deterioration** (1 Kings 14:21–31). Rehoboam reigned over Judah during 931–913 BC. His mother was evidently an important figure (14:21), but she was not an Israelite. Solomon's marrying foreign women meant that his son, Rehoboam, now king of Judah, was only half-Israelite and had reasons for being sympathetic to paganism. It is not totally surprising that Rehoboam continued Solomon's idolatry (14:22).

Without an intervention of God any nation will slip into ever-increasing depravity. Even Judah, despite all that had happened in its past, moves steadily into greater and greater sin. *'They provoked Him to jealousy more than all that their fathers had done'* (14:22). In addition to the idolatry there came into Judean society more 'high places'. The heirs of David were doing no better than the breakaway northerners. Also, in Rehoboam's day 'sacred pillars' were built, upright standing stones representing male gods, forbidden by the law (Exodus 23:24; Deuteronomy 16:22). And they were building 'Asherim' or 'Asherahs', images of a Canaanite mother-goddess (14:23). The law demanded they be cut down (Exodus 24:13) or burned (Deuteronomy 12:3). They introduced the vile Canaanite practise of 'holy' prostitution in which men and women were used for immoral purposes at the various centres of pagan 'worship' (14:24). God's law had forbidden that centuries before (Deuteronomy 23:18).

The situation is getting progressively worse. This is how it will always be unless God's grace is at work, and sin will have its consequences. Judah will soon lose the prosperity that was built up by Solomon if the nation does not walk in the ways of God. Shishak (or 'Shoshenq') of Egypt invaded Israel (14:25). Solomon's accumulated treasures were lost (14:26); bronze shields replaced gold shields (14:27–28). Although Shishak was not able to permanently control Israel, the nation's finances were severely reduced. Also there was continual war with northern Israel (14:29–30). Rehoboam's death was sufficiently honourable as to allow him to be buried in the city of David (14:31) but nothing of any spiritual value had been achieved in his reign. It had been a story of deepening decline.

2. **The lesson of Abijam's reign is: no spiritual advance can come unless favourite sins are repudiated** (15:1–8). Abijam reigned over Judah for only three years (15:1–2a), during 913–910 BC. Again the 'queen mother' continued to be a powerful person (15:2b). Again he continued in idolatrous ways. Hostility between north and south continued. He died after reigning only three years, without achieving anything notable! Abijam is dismissed with few words, none of them encouraging. The account in 2 Chronicles 13 reveals more about him and we discover he could be very enthusiastic about the traditions of Jerusalem, but none of that changed the fact that *'his heart was not loyal to the LORD'* (15:3). It was only because God had sworn an oath to David

concerning his life that the kingship (like a continually burning lamp) was allowed to continue in his line (15:4–5).

What a tragedy it is in any area of life when years go by and no improvement is made in relation to God. Abijam's three years were busy (as 15:6, 7 and 2 Chronicles 13 shows) but the amount of spiritual advance that was made was nil. Abijam inherited a wicked idolatry from Rehoboam and he simply kept things the way they were. He received an honourable burial (15:8) but it had not been an honourable reign.

3. **The lesson of Asa's reign is: spirituality will bring blessing but if real progress is to be made it must be maintained to the very end** (15:9–24). Asa's days were a time of partial spiritual recovery. He reigned over Judah for about 40 years, during 910–869 BC, sharing the rule with his son as joint-king during the last three years (872–869 BC). His grandmother continued in power as 'queen mother' (15:9–10; see 15:2). Asa was the first of eight kings of Judah (Asa, Jehoshaphat, Joash, Amaziah, Azariah, Jotham, Hezekiah, Josiah) who are described favourably by 1 and 2 Kings (15:11).

He started well. He was willing to get rid of inherited wickedness. He removed the cult-prostitutes (15:12). It must have been difficult to remove his grand-mother from power, but he was willing to do whatever was needed to restore the country (15:13).

Yet these days of spiritual blessing did not entirely turn the tide. Asa did not remove the high places (15:14). Nothing would ever bring about the recovery of Judah unless the 'high places' were taken away and the nation turned away from idolatry for ever!

His godliness was seen in his willingness to deposit spoils of war in the temple (15:15) but then a crisis came. He experienced war with Israel (15:16) throughout his reign. A breakdown in his life came when Baasha, king of Israel, built a fort at Ramah (15:17) only a few miles from Jerusalem. This was very threatening and Asa turned to Syria for help (15:18). Syria or Aram was a powerful empire which had its capital in Damascus and became powerful after the death of Solomon in about 930 BC. It had a line of kings who are mentioned in 1 Kings, including Rezon (955–925 BC approximately), Hezion (925–915 BC approximately), Tabrimmon (915–900 BC approximately), Ben-Hadad I (900–860 approximately), Ben-Hadad II (860–843 approximately) Hazael (843–796) and Ben-Hadad III (796–770 BC).

Asa paid a large bribe to Ben-Hadad I (15:18–19) and thus persuaded them to attack Israel (15:20). The Israelites abandoned the fortress in Ramah (15:21). Asa was acting in unbelief, trusting a pagan neighbour but not trusting God. The miraculous deliverances of the days of David were no longer experienced, for David's descendants lacked his faith. The Judeans dismantled Ramah (15:22). Asa's later years were clouded by disease (15:23). He was given an honourable burial in David's city (15:24). Asa was a good king but not good enough to turn the situation around altogether.

Chapter 24

Idolatry and Society
(1 Kings 15:25–16:28)

Now the writer of 1 Kings turns from Judah to the story of the northern kingdom.

The central lesson of 1 Kings 15:25–16:28 is that **idolatry has a corrupting effect in society**. There are five kings mentioned here.

1. **Nadab of Israel (1 Kings 15:25–31) was assassinated**. He reigned during 909–908 BC and continued the ways of his father Jeroboam (15:25–26). He was without God's approval or protection. In the middle of a battle he was assassinated (15:27–28) and the entire family of Jeroboam was exterminated (15:29–30). This fulfilled the prophecy of Ahijah. The narrator's last sentence about him (15:31) does not tell us that he *'lay with his fathers'*. His violent end meant that he had no honourable burial.

2. **Baasha of Israel (1 Kings 15;33–16:7 had the opportunity of reversing Jeroboam's sins but he did not take the opportunity**. He started a second line of kings, unrelated to Jeroboam, and reigned during 908–866 BC. Like all the kings of northern Israel, he continued to maintain the idolatrous religion Jeroboam had started (15:33–34). Yet because he was the founder of a new line of kings he had the opportunity to do something new. A prophet called Jehu brought him a message (16:1; he was no relation to the later Jehu son of Jehoshaphat). It was God who had allowed him to become king (*'I raised you from the dust'*, 16:2) but

Baasha did not take the opportunity of reform and he would follow the same route as Jeroboam (16:3–4). Despite his works of greatness (16:5) he achieved nothing for God. The final comments tell us of his burial at Tirzeh (the first time we are told the place where a northern king was buried, 16:6). The major event of his reign was that he received a prophecy but did nothing about it (16:7).

3. **Elah of Israel (1 Kings 16:8–14) was a drunk who repeated history**. He reigned during 886–885 BC, but his short reign never achieved anything worthwhile. Almost as soon as he came on the throne, while he was in a drunken state, one of his commanders assassinated him (16:8–10). The new king Zimri, did to his family exactly what he and his father had done to Jeroboam's family. History repeated itself. Baasha and Elah were not able to rise above Jeroboam and his son Nadab (16:11). As the prophet had brought a prophecy to Jeroboam, so Jehu brought the same prophecy to Baasha (16:12). Both were fulfilled. The story of Baasha and Elah was exactly parallel to the story of Jeroboam and Nadab. This time the writer traces the cause not to Jeroboam's sin but to their own sins (16:13–14). He introduces a word he has not used before, *'vain things'*. Father and son, Baasha and Elah, were preoccupied with pagan gods and so achieved nothing for Israel. It is obvious that there is a rapid downward trend in Israelite society.

4. **Zimri of Israel(1 Kings 16:15–22) is notable for having a seven-day reign (16:15a) in 885 BC before committing suicide**. He had assassinated the previous king during a time of conflict against a town called Gibbethon (16:15b). His was the third new start in Israel but the people immediately made Omri the king (16:16) and supported Omri in his besieging Gibbethon (16:17). Omri was the general of the entire army. Zimri was only the commander of the chariot-force. Apparently Zimri was ambitious to rise higher in power and position than the general of the army. The army did not support Zimri's ambition and Omri would obviously soon get rid of Zimri. So Zimri saw that his future was doomed and killed himself, destroying the king's house at

the same time (16:18). He had been a follower of Jeroboam's idolatry (16:19) and was not willing to turn to the God of Israel for help. Chaos followed these events and for a while there was civil war between Timni and Omri, but Omri emerged as the new king (16:20–22).

5. **Omri of Israel (1 Kings 16:23–28) was famous amongst ancient kings but had no significance in the progress of God's kingdom**. He reigned during 885–874 BC and started a fourth dynasty (line of kings). He spent five years in civil war with Timni. After his victory over Timni he transferred his capital from Tirzeh to Samaria and so the northern kingdom becomes 'Samaria' (16:23–24). During his reign the downward trend continued. To Jeroboam's sins he added his own (16:25–26). The Assyrians spoke of Israel as 'the land of Omri', but 1 Kings dismisses him speedily (16:27–28).

A religion that promotes immorality and licentiousness cannot be the base for a strong community. The story of northern Israel so far has been full of conspiracies and violence. No king arises who has a love for God which will set him on the path to reform. The king determines the character of the kingdom. If the king is wicked and corrupt he spreads wickedness and corruption in his kingdom. 1 Kings is about the establishing of kingdoms. The answer to the various needs that are presented is a new 'Son of David'. He is the only one whose kingly power will ever bring into being what the narrative of 1 Kings is looking for. Only Jesus will ever be a full 'Son of David'. One day a King will come of whom it can be said *'Righteousness will be the sceptre of your kingdom. You have loved righteousness and hated wickedness'* (Hebrews 1:8–9). Then the character of the King will again determine the character of the kingdom. Idolatry produce a throne that cannot last. Only when there comes a righteous Son of David will it be said *'Your throne ... will last for ever and ever'* (Hebrews 1:8).

Chapter 25

Finding Courage
(1 Kings 16:29–17:24)

We reach the reign of Ahab, king of northern Israel during 874–853 BC (16:29) and the wickedest king in Israel to this point (16:30). He *'sold himself to do evil'* (1 Kings 21:25), and almost wiped out of existence the faith of Israel. He was influenced by a wife who encouraged him in a life of extreme wickedness (1 Kings 21:25–26), driving him to go back to the Canaanite worship that had originally caused God to punish them at the time Israel entered into the land of Canaan (21:26).

Solomon had tolerated the worship of foreign gods. Jeroboam had for political reasons set up golden calves to be worshipped. Ahab went further still. He worshipped Baal and made Baal-worship the national religion (1 Kings 18:4, 19). He hated prophets like Elijah and Micaiah (1 Kings 18:17; 22:8) and murdered many of the Lord's prophets (1 Kings 18:13). Baal was the fertility god of the Canaanites. He was thought to have control over wind and rain and clouds, and so over fertility. It was in the days of Ahab that Baal-worship became worse than ever.

Jezebel came from the Phoenician territory of Sidon (16:31b). Ahab and Jezebel built a temple for Baal (16:31b–32) and made an *'Asherah-pole'*, an upright statue designed to represent another goddess of fertility (16:33). It was in Ahab's days that Jericho, an ancient pagan city, was rebuilt (16:34).

Elijah was God's man for the hour, a man that God raised up to uphold the message of God in a time of great opposition towards His kingdom. Elijah will help us to find boldness and courage, for the Bible tells us that he was an ordinary person (James 5:17) but that he learned great lessons of prayer. God raised his faith to extraordinary heights. He was able to ask God to send drought for over three years. He was the first person ever to pray for the dead to be raised and see his prayer answered. He was *'a man with a nature like ours'* but *'he prayed . . . '.*

In the narrative of 1 Kings, Elijah appears suddenly. He is a picture of the kind of person needed in this world, a model of courage, a model of a ministry that restores the work of God (see Matthew 17:10–12; Malachi 3:10).

1. **Elijah is a man with great courage and boldness that comes from being in the will of God** (17:1–6).

His courage came from his call. Elijah appears as a man with a call from God. He dramatically appears on the scene (17:1). We do not read of his genealogy or background. Kings and priests need to have a genealogy. They inherit their power or their priesthood from their ancestry. But a prophet is different. Only a call from God makes a prophet. It does not matter where he comes from. It only matters that he is here. He seems to drop from heaven like an angel but he is in fact just like us! Every Christian has a call. One's background is not all that important although God will use it.

His courage came from his knowledge of God's will. Elijah appears as a man who knows God's will and can bring about God's will. He knows God's will in prayer and is able to speak with certainty because he knows his prayer has been answered. He knows it will not rain for three years. He knows God will answer his prayers concerning the weather. He was a man just like us, yet he prayed. He predicted a drought because he had the assurance that God would hear his prayers. He told the king, Ahab. The judgement was the result of Elijah's praying.

He was a man who knew God. *'Before whom I stand'.* He

was able to stand before Ahab because he had previously stood before God.

His courage came from God's directions in his life. His comings and goings were under God's control. God sent him to Ahab (17:1). God sent him to the Kerith Ravine (17:2–3). Water is provided for him by a stream. Food is miraculously supplied by ravens (17:4). He obeys the Lord (17:5) and finds God fulfils His promise (17:6).

His courage came from God's provision. Elijah appears as a man who is provided for by God.

2. **Elijah is a man who is used to ministering to others** (17:7–16). A change in God's will for Elijah's life appears. For some time he dwelt near Kerith while the drought was taking place. Then the brook dries up; he must leave Kerith (17:7). At first it seems to be a disaster. God's provision has ended. But He raises up another means of provision. He is sent to Zarephath in Sidon. God can protect us anywhere! He gave Elijah protection in the very country of the wicked queen who must have hated him (17:8–9; see 16:31), Sidon is in the midst of idolatry. It would deepen his conviction about the evil of Sidon. Elijah meets the woman he is sent to, who is in extreme destitution (17:10). He tests her by asking for water in a time of drought (17:10b). Then he adds to the burden by asking for bread (17:11). She confesses her desperation; she is about to eat her last meal (17:12) but has been willing to help a prophet (17:10a). If she continues in this life of faithfulness she will find endless provision during the time of need (17:13–14). She finds God to be true to His word (17:15–16).

3. **Elijah is a man who is proved through answered prayer** (17:17–24). The woman of Zarephath is a Sidonian. Yet she has faith in the God of Israel. It is not a very strong faith (as we are about to see) but is is real and it is sincere. God has chosen to bless her.

In the midst of her life of ministry to Elijah there suddenly comes a crisis. The woman's son dies (17:17) and in the weakness of her faith the woman becomes bitterly angry and full of guilt-feelings (17:18). At the same time Elijah faces a nasty accusation. But Elijah's way of vindicating himself is to pray. He takes the boy (17:19), prays (17:20), and persistently seeks to impart life to him (17:21). Elijah is heard (17:22), the boy lives, and is given to his mother (17:23). This vindicates his ministry (17:24).

Chapter 26

Elijah, Obadiah, Ahab

(1 Kings 18:1–17)

Elijah is led by the Lord to swing around the entire nation for God. It is to be done not so much by teaching as by prayer-power. The first thing he must do is demonstrate that it is the LORD and not Baal who is in control of fertility. He was led to pray that 'the LORD the God of Israel' would withhold fertility for three years. So sure is he that prayer has been answered he announces the drought to Ahab (17:1). It demonstrates the uselessness of Baal in the matter of fertility! It shows that the LORD can give prosperity or can turn a land into a desert! Often spiritual battles have to be fought by prayer-power.

Elijah makes his announcement and then stays hidden for three years, first at Kerith, then at Zarephath. Then the Lord tells Elijah that the time for the end of the drought is at hand (18:1).

There are three personalities in 1 Kings 18. First see **the massive foresight and the dramatic courage of Elijah.**

1. **He has to move under the direction of God.** God gives him instructions about his movements, and he is told he must appear before Ahab again. God plans to send rain and Elijah's work must take a step forward (18:1). What had Elijah been doing in these years? Probably seeking God's will and power.

2. **He has to be willing to leave aside earthly comforts.** He had been at Kerith perhaps for a year, but then had gone to

a more comfortable life with the widow of Zarephath. Now three and a half years of drought have gone by (see James 5:17) and Elijah has had over two years of ease in peaceful fellowship with the widow of Zarephath who, as a believer in pagan Sidon, had been a support and a companion to him. While Israel and the surrounding territories had been in the midst of drought and famine, God had supplied Elijah and his widowed friend with enough to eat and Elijah's whereabouts had been unknown. Now he has to leave Zarephath to go to find Ahab (18:2). It was to be at Elijah's word (see 17:1) that the drought would end. It was to be made obvious that the beginning and end of the drought was not the work of Baal but was the result of the decision of God, announced through His prophet. But not everyone is called to such dramatic courage.

The second character in the story is **Obadiah, a man of steady faithfulness who lived for God in most difficult circumstances**. His calling in life was to work in the palace for Ahab. He was led to be a godly man working in an ungodly place (18:3a). He must not be thought to be a compromiser. He feared the Lord greatly (18:3), having come to know the LORD when he was young, and having followed the LORD for many years. God had put him in a place of special advantage and he had been used by God to protect His prophets. On one occasion he had risked his life to protect a hundred of the Lord's prophets (18:4). It was in the course of his faithful work for Ahab (18:5–6) that he met Elijah and was asked to send a message to Ahab (18:7–8).

However Elijah was known for his unexpected appearances and disappearances (18:9–14)! Before Obadiah will agree to pass a message on to Ahab he requires an oath from Elijah that he will not disappear again (18:15–16). Elijah has evaded capture for over three years. If Ahab discovers that Obadiah is used by Elijah as a friend the life of Obadiah will be in danger.

Obadiah was like Daniel who worked for the pagan king Nebuchadnezzar. There are people who are called not to be 'full-time ministers' in the work of God, but are called to be adminstrators or workers in government. Obadiah was not a prophet like Elijah, yet he was able to use his position in the court of Ahab to help God's people (18:4). The work he did was not sinful. There was a lot of wickedness around him because of the activities of Ahab and Jezebel, but he himself used his position for God. God needs Elijahs but He needs Obadiahs as well.

The third character of the story is **Ahab, who continues in wickedness and spiritual blindness**. He employs a godly man, Obadiah, as his steward and assistant. The very godliness that Ahab is persecuting is what makes Obadiah such a faithful worker. Ungodly men find that godly men are the best employees!

In the midst of drought Ahab is only concerned about finding places of green pasture to keep his animals alive (18:5). He regards Elijah as only a trouble maker (18:17) and is blind to the fact that the drought has been brought on Israel by his own sinful worship of Baal. What is the good of worshipping a god of fertility if that god of fertility cannot stop three years drought? After three years one might think that Ahab would realise that worshipping the god of fertility does not do any good for the fertility of the land.

Elijah is risking his life – it might seem – in presenting himelf to Ahab. He might be immediately killed as many other prophets have been killed. But Elijah knows he is in the hands of God and is not afraid. Ahab, for his part, was told that the drought would end only at the word of Elijah. He has become convinced that this is true and has been searching for Elijah over the course of the last three years. So it is not likely he will kill him now that he has found him but before the drought has ended. Elijah's word is the only hope he has of the drought coming to an end.

The ministry of Elijah is a ministry of restoration. The faith of Israel had been almost annihilated. Elijah's task was to swing everything around to God again. *'Elijah will restore everything'*, said Jesus (Mark 9:12). John the Baptist was another Elijah-figure. He had great boldness, like Elijah. He did not care about the opinions of people. Elijah could dramatically appear and then disappear for three years. He was not looking for publicity. John the Baptist was the same kind of person. He too could live in a desert just as Elijah could live by a stream in a deep valley.

There are times in the story of the church when God needs people who care nothing for their own reputation, who put God before any of the world's comforts, who have power with God in prayer, *'power to shut the sky'* (Revelation 11:6). Then the Ahabs of this world have to listen, and God's Elijah is able to swing the entire situation around for God and *'restore everything'*.

Chapter 27

When the Gods Fail

(1 Kings 18:18–32)

There are times in the work of the Lord where what is needed is not teaching or instruction or discussion but mighty acts of God's power. There come times in the story of the church where the gospel is almost overwhelmed. The days of Ahab were such a time, and Elijah was raised up to meet the need. We do not know anything about the life of Elijah before 1 Kings 17:1, but it is clear that he was not an immature beginner in the things of God. A man who can pray for a dead child to come to life with confidence and assurance and see it happen is probably not a newcomer to the things of prayer and faith.

I suppose there were years of experience before that day when he stood before Ahab and announced that it would not rain for three years. And then we can be sure that his two years or more with the widow of Zaraphath, although they may have been restful, were not days of idleness. Elijah had had much time to think and prepare for this day when he would swing around the entire spiritual mood of the nation of Israel.

Now the day had come. He challenged Ahab to a contest. Ahab was to pray to his gods of fertility. Elijah was to pray to the LORD, the God of Israel. Elijah was a prophet. He was walking close to God. God was not doing anything without telling Elijah his prophet (see Amos 3:7). The prophet had been in fellowship with the Lord and God had revealed to him some things that were to happen.

Not everyone can do this kind of thing, and there are many who are 'playing the game of being a prophet'. I have known many people who have claimed that God is telling them what He is doing, but I have not known many whose claims I have believed – only a few. A prophet is a person who has *'stood in the council of the LORD to perceive and to hear his word'* (Jeremiah 23:18).

But Elijah was not playing a game, and his life would be lost if his predictions did not come to pass. He challenged Ahab to a 'prayer-contest' and said *'The God who proves himself – He is God!'* He said to Ahab 'Your god is useless. You have brought the country into disaster by forsaking the only true God (see 18:18). Now let us have a contest. You gather your pagan prophets of Baal, the male god of fertility, and of Asherah, the female god of fertility and let us find out who is the true God' (see 18:19). It is not the kind of thing you do unless you are sure God is leading you, but there are times when we are led to know that God is about to 'answer by fire'.

Ahab does what Elijah asks (18:20). A massive crowd gathers and Elijah addresses 'the people' (18:21). The nation of Israel had been deceived by Ahab and Jezebel. It was time that 'the people' should discover the truth. The same is true in many modern parts of the world. How many places there are where 'the people' have false gods, false religions, even phoney and fake versions of the Christian faith. It is about time 'the people' were told the truth. The only God is the God of the Bible, the inspired and infallible Word of God. The only way of salvation is by the blood-atonement of Jesus. The only power that can powerfully change lives is the power of the Holy Spirit. Heaven is real; hell is real. Every member of the human race is destined for heaven or for hell. It is time we abandoned these fake religions and turned to the one and only Saviour.

Elijah asks the people to make up their minds. *'How long will you go around limping on two crutches?'* (18:21). The people say nothing. They have got used to the national religion of Baal-worship.

Elijah explains the 'prayer-contest'. It is four hundred and fifty versus one (18:22)! A sacrifice is to be prepared but no fire is to be lit (18:23). Then the people and the prophets of Baal can call upon Baal and Elijah will call upon God. *'The God who answers by fire, He is God'* (18:24).

The contest begins. The prophets of Baal start (18:25). Elijah is about to demonstrate the uselessness of false religion.

The lessons of the contest become apparent. Pagan praying takes a long time. These phony gods were called on from morning to evening (18:26).

Pagan praying requires a lot of ritual. These phoney prophets leaped about the altar performing some kind of ceremonial dance (18:26). It did not do any good. These prophets were not in touch with any real God who had any real power above the God of Israel. Elijah gets sarcastic. *'You should shout a bit louder. Make a lot of noise. Perhaps your god has fallen asleep and you need to wake him up. Maybe he is busy at the moment'* (18:27).

Pagan praying often involves self-inflicted suffering. These prophets of Baal cut themselves and lashed themselves until the blood flowed out (18:28). Apparently they felt that their god required a lot of physical sacrifice before he would answer them.

Who were these gods anyway? Who were 'Baal' and 'Asherah'? They were inventions of the human imagination. They were man-made fantasies. The difference between all religions and the faith of the Bible is that man-made philosophies are 'discovered' by research or they are 'invented' by someone who has a religious theory. But the God of the Bible is a God who has **revealed** himself. We believe what we believe because He has stepped into the history of the world in Jesus. He has stepped into our lives and revealed Himself by His Holy Spirit. The Christian faith is not philosophy. It is not religiosity. It is not religious ceremony.

These gods were encouragers of wickedness. How much sin and wickedness came into Israel because of Baal and Asherah! Man-made religions and man-made gods never lead to holy living.

These gods let you down when you need them. *'There was no voice, no one answered, and no one paid attention'* (18:29).

We Christians need to be careful that we do not adopt a version of the Christian faith that is more pagan than Christian. The God of the Bible is not a God of ritual or religiosity. He is the One and Only God, the Father of Jesus, the One who is approached by the blood of Jesus, the God who answers by fire when we find Him for ourselves.

Chapter 28

Looking for the Fire to Fall

(1 Kings 18:31–46)

Elijah is now led by God to show that the Lord is real.

1. **Led by God, Elijah takes the initiative**. God is restoring His people. He directs Elijah to act boldly and to take steps at His initiative. The situation is not in the hands of Ahab or the false prophets. It is in the hands of God and His prophet.

2. **Elijah demands that the altar be rebuilt first**. He demands that the entire nation get back to God and His promised gospel. The altar symbolises God's way of salvation by blood-atonement. It reminded the Israelites of the passover lamb and it reminds modern Christians of the blood of Jesus. The way of salvation is not through exhausting religious routine. It is not through ceremony. It is by faith in the sin-bearing sacrifice of Jesus.

3. If the nation is to be blessed, **these northern Israelites must remember God's original promises to the nation**. Elijah takes twelve stones representing the entire people of God, not just northern Israel where Ahab is king (18:31). It recalls the twelve pillars Moses built when the law was being given to all Israel (Exodus 24:4). The whole nation entered the land and Joshua took twelve stones from the Jordan and made a memorial out of them at Gilgal (Joshua 4:3–7, 19), a reminder that *'the hand of the LORD is mighty'* and that He is to be revered for ever (Joshua 4:24).

4. **Elijah makes it clear that there is nothing manipulated here** (18:31–35). Spiritual renewal often has in it a touch of

the miraculous and Elijah knows that fire is to fall from heaven. He wants to make it perfectly clear that what is about to happen is not a trick but sheer intervention by God. The days we live in are days of world-wide charismatic renewal but we would do well to follow Elijah's example and take steps to make it clear to everyone that nothing we do is manipulated.

5. **Elijah makes it clear that he is taking the nation back to obedience to the Mosaic law, which was God's will for the nation before the giving of the Spirit**. He waits for the time of the evening sacrifice (18:36). He authenticates the revelation of God at the time of Moses. He witnesses to the God who had given promises to Abraham, Isaac and Jacob (18:36). He asks to be authenticated himself (18:36). He asks that God may act in such a way that they know that He is powerfully bringing revival and restoration to Israel (18:37).

6. **Then there comes a powerful action of God that persuades the people** (18:38–39). The fire falls, and the people collapse forwards on their faces (not backwards!) before God. False prophets were executed (18:40). Putting it in modern terms: false gospels were put down and the one and only message of the gospel was vindicated. There had just been three-and-a-half years of judgement upon the nation because of its worship of Baal. But Elijah is being used by God to turn the nation round.

Now it is time for the judgement of God to end and the blessings of God to return. Elijah prays for rain. We notice some principles in his praying.

1. **Praying for great things has to take into account God's timing**. In this case no spiritual blessings can come to Israel until sins have been put aside. A preliminary to prayer is putting idols away. When the people had got right with the Lord the time for restoration of blessing had arrived.

Elijah was used by God to swing round the nation of Israel to the Lord. First he announces three years without rain (17:1). Then he disappears for three years in the valley of Kerith, and then with the widow of Zarephath. Then he shows himself to Ahab and challenges him to a

126

prayer-contest. The prophets of Baal are slaughtered. Now it is time for the three year drought to be finished.

2. **Prayer has to be in faith, a faith based on what God has said**. 1 Kings 18:41 seems to mean 'Go and have a meal. Don't worry about the drought. I can hear the sound of a mighty rain-fall'. The prayer-contest is finished. 'There is going to be very heavy rain. I can hear it coming!' This tells us of the nature of faith. Faith sees what cannot be seen. Faith hears what cannot be heard. It is the substance of things that are not there yet. But it is based on what God has previously said to us. Elijah asks for what God has promised.

3. **Elijah prays with deep reverence** (18:42). He shows great respect for God, great dependence. He needs further help and guidance from God.

4. **Elijah prays with expectation and persistence** (18:43). He is looking for the thing that he is praying for. He goes on and on until it comes.

5. **He recognizes the answer when it first begins**. He acts upon what he knows is just about to happen. He says to Ahab 'You had better get moving. The rain is going to be so heavy your chariot wheels will get stuck if you do not move soon' (18:44). Soon the rain begins to pour (18:45).

6. **The answer to prayer brings joy and physical energy**. In the power of the Lord's special enabling, Elijah runs 27 kilometres, so fast that he gets to Jezreel before Ahab. Jezreel is the place where Ahab's palace is. What is happening is the physical side-effect of great anointing. When the power of the Lord is present in one's life it gives unusual physical drive. He was perhaps honouring Ahab. He wanted to present the victory at Jezreel. Perhaps he hoped to win round Jezebel.

When God's fire falls everyone gets added confirmation that God is real.

Chapter 29

Elijah's Self-Pity

(1 Kings 19:1–21)

Elijah has been doing some wonderful things since we first see a mention of him in 1 Kings 17:1. For several years he was involved in swinging the entire nation around for God. He announces that it will not rain for some years (17:1), then disappears and stays at Kerith (17:2–6) and Zarephath. There was the miracle of the woman's endless provision and Elijah's raising her son from the dead (17:7–24). The climax of it all comes on Mount Carmel. After three years he arranges to meet Ahab (18:1–16), demands that he summon the prophets of Baal for a contest (18:17–24), calls for fire from heaven (18:25–39) and slaughters the prophets of Baal (18:40). After that he promises rain and it comes (18:41–46). It has been an amazing, a dramatic and an exciting few years.

Now Elijah experiences a violent swing of mood and suddenly we find Elijah in the depths of depression.

First, we consider how the believer may be overcome by unbelief. Elijah is famous for his faith. He could even pray and *'have power to shut up the sky so that it will not rain'* (Revelation 11:6). Yet this man of God is attacked by unbelief. He was overcome by a violent attack of depression. He was afraid. Although before he had boldly confronted Ahab (18:17–18, 40) now we are told *'He was afraid and arose and ran'* (This translation is better than the KJV, *'And he saw'*.) He fled to a different country

(*'Beersheba, which belongs to Judah'*). He left his servant (19:3), wanting to be alone, and overcome by depression he asked to die. It was violent attack of unbelief. This can happen to God's people. We can be attacked by a spirit of unbelief. When we are doing great things for God, beyond our ability, suddenly we are shown the greatness of what we are doing and are overcome by fear.

Secondly, let us consider the causes of this attack of depression. It has more than one cause. There is a reason in the spiritual world. Jezebel is an evil woman, a worshipper of pagan gods. Anyone who confronts her is likely to find he is struggling not against flesh and blood but against spiritual forces of wickedness.

There was a physical aspect to it and a pyschological aspect to it. We have just been told that Elijah's victory on Mount Carmel brought physical exuberance. Elijah had run 27 kilometres, so fast that he got to Jezreel before Ahab. Anyone who has been experiencing such excitements and enduring strains and stresses, is likely to experience a reaction in which he swings from exuberance to depression.

There was a cause in Elijah's temperament. He was an ambitious person. Many of God's Elijahs are ambitious people determined to achieve something with their lives. Elijah complained *'I am not better than my fathers'*. It is a very revealing remark! He wanted to outclass what others had done before him.

He was a man of faith but at this point he was failing to apply his faith. Sometimes the Lord has to ask us 'Where is your faith?' We may be people of faith but then in a time of crisis we may forget to apply our faith. We may start walking on the waters and then suddenly be overcome with the sight of the waves.

Thirdly, we consider the way God restored him. He did not reject His servant. He sent an angel to minister to Elijah's health. He was allowed to sleep and eat (19:5–8). A physical problem may need a physical answer. Jesus may say to us *'come apart and rest awhile'*. Certainly he is concerned about our physical needs.

Then God gave Elijah some encouraging revelations. God gently rebuked his self-pity (*'What are you doing here?'* 1 Kings 19:9). Elijah had a pessimistic estimate of the situation he was in (19:10). God then brought three mighty sets of physical phenomena before Elijah (19:11–12a) but God did not appear in any of these dramatic phenomena! It was an overwhelming demonstration of God's power. Elijah felt the presence of God and covered his face. Then there came a gentle blowing wind (19:12b) in which a voice spoke to him (19:13). It was God's way of saying that He works in quiet ways as well as in dramatic ways.

God tells him He can take care of His church and He has the future already under His control. He must anoint three people (19:14–15). He must anoint Hazael king of Syria. Hazael would later be a judgement upon Israel's idolatry. He must anoint Jehu who would be another instrument of judgement upon the nation. And he must anoint Elisha who will not only execute judgement upon false prophets but also will be Elijah's successor (19:16–17). God also corrects Elijah's false estimate of the situation. There are seven thousand who are loyal to him (19:18).

Elisha's call comes as Elijah throws his mantle over him. It is a remarkably subtle call. It puts all of the responsibility upon Elisha. It is as if Elijah is saying 'Do you want to be my successor? I am giving you the opportunity if you like' (19:19). When Elisha asks for further instruction (19:20), Elijah says in effect 'Do whatever you want to' (19:20). The call comes to Elisha in the middle of his ordinary work, but he takes the hint, uses the wood of his ploughing instrument to make a fire, uses the oxen to make a whole burnt offering, offers himself to God (19:21), and starts his training immediately as Elijah's understudy (19:21). Elijah now has an assistant. His spell of depression is ended.

Chapter 30

Keeping the Armour On
(1 Kings 20:1–22)

We come to an occasion when Ahab goes out to battle in a
country to the north of Israel ruled by Ben-Hadad the
second. We have had an earlier Ben-Hadad, who was his
father (1 Kings 15:18). Ben-Hadad II comes with a mighty
army and surrounds Samaria, the capital of the northern
territory of Israel (20:1). With great arrogance he demands
the wealth and the women and children of Ahab (20:2–3).
Ahab is overwhelmed and feels he has no choice but to
submit (20:4). The idolatry of Israel has led to steady deterioration in the country's power. Solomon had once received
gifts from surrounding nations, but now surrounding
nations want gifts from Israel.

Then Ben-Hadad increases his demand. He now wants to
search Ahab's palace and strip Ahab and his senior officials
of every last remnant of their possessions (20:5–6).

This time Ahab consults his men and refuses (20:7–9) and
Ben-Hadad threatens to entirely destroy Samaria (20:10)
but Ahab still will not yield (20:11). Ben-Hadad prepares to
invade (20:12). A prophet encourages Ahab that he will be
given victory, and he is given detailed guidance (20:13–14).
Ahab follows the prophetic advice (20:15). Ben-Hadad and
his men are indulging themselves when Ahab and his men
approach (20:16–17a) but are still full of self-confidence
(20:17b–18). Ahab and his men continue to follow the
guidance of the prophet and are given victory (20:19–20a).

Ben-Hadad escapes; Ahab is leading the army as instructed by the prophet (20:20b–21a). The result is a great victory (20:21b).

1. **It comes as a surprise that God is willing to help Ahab at all!** He is a wicked king, no better than Ben-Hadad. Why should God be willing to help Ahab? Yet God has not forsaken northern Israel. He had taken the whole of the country of Israel to be His people. Although His original land has divided into northern Israel and the south, Judah, yet God still regards the whole nation as His people. He is more gracious and patient than one might imagine. He does not deal with His people as their sins deserve. The gospel of our Lord Jesus is a gospel of grace. Often God's grace takes us by surprise. Often God is gracious to people whom we feel He ought not to be gracious to at all.

2. **God has a hatred of self-confident pride**. What arrogance and boastfulness is shown by Ben-Hadad. How self-confident he is in his demands. How careless and lazy he is back at the army headquarters. He thinks he can easily subdue Samaria. But God has a hatred of such pride. And God has a habit of reducing such self-confident arrogance to humiliation.

3. **The story is also a study in prophetic guidance**. The prophet gives quite detailed advice to Ahab and his advice is followed carefully in the battle. Modern churches need to get used to the idea of finding God's will by prophetic guidance. There is every reason to think that the church of Jesus Christ is still to have prophets. Of course there are many difficulties and churches that follow 'prophets' often go astray. But we must not be so intimidated by difficulties that we reject prophecy altogether because of its difficulties. Handled wisely and sensibly there is still a need for prophetic guidance in the church of Jesus Christ.

It is best if prophetic guidance is supported by the prayerful seeking of God's will by the whole leadership (as in Acts 13) where an entire team of leaders are seeking God's will. One will be cautious about any guidance that seems odd or bizarre. Any person who regularly leads the church in prophetic ministry must be tested. His help should be carefully noted and what comes as a result of following it.

Prophetic guidance should be carefully considered. It often comes as a surprise and yet when it is carefully considered there is often visible wisdom in it. In this case one can see the wisdom of the prophetic advice. The older leaders were discouraged and intimidated. The prophet's advice was to send the *'young servants'* (the Hebrew means this) of the provincial governors of Israel. These younger, more energetic men, were put at the front of the battle. God gave them wisdom. They came at a time when Ben-Hadad and his men were exceptionally ill-prepared. God gave them victory.

4. **The story reminds us that one phase of battle prepares us for the next phase of battle.** The prophet comes back again with a warning that there is more to come before Ahab can relax (20:22). The advice given to Ben-Hadad (20:14), *'Let not him who puts his armour on boast like him who takes his armour off'*, applies to Ahab as well! And it applies to us. Let us not think we have victory until everything is thoroughly accomplished. The battle seems to be over, but Ahab is warned *'Go strengthen yourself'*. There is more to come. We sometimes think that a period of conflict is over when the truth is that everything we have been through is only preparation.

Ahab's victory must not make him self-confident. In any project for God we have to move humbly, not making claims to great ability or great knowledge. God will give us guidance along the way. Some of it may be surprising but if we follow tenderly at His leading, God will bring us through every crisis. One day the battle will be ended, and we will be able to put our armour off altogether. At the moment we are still in the battle.

Chapter 31

Misguided Mercy
(1 Kings 20:23–43)

Ben-Hadad II had surrounded Samaria, demanding the wealth and the women and children of Ahab. Helped by detailed guidance, Ahab was rescued and given victory over Ben-Hadad (20:1–21), but the prophet warned him that he would face another attack in the following year (20:22).

Ben-Hadad's military advisers are convinced that their defeat came about only because they chose the incorrect area in which to fight. Their gods are gods of the plains; they lost because they fought in the hills (20:23)! Here we have a picture of gods with limited areas of supervision! Ben-Hadad's advisors have not grasped that the God of Israel is the God of the universe with no area which is out of His reach and control.

Also Ben-Hadad follows a new method. Instead of using kings he uses commanders (20:24). A new army was mobilized and victory was thought to be on its way (20:25). A great army faced Israel, whereas Israel itself had only a small army *like two little flocks of goats'* (20:26–27).

Once again a prophet comes and gives help and Israel is victorious (20:28–30a).

Ben-Hadad II is trapped and is about to be captured (20:30b). His men urge him to ask for mercy (20:31–32a) and Ahab is flattered. *'He is my brother'*, he says with seemingly great magnanimity (20:32b) and Ben-Hadad is brought out (20:33). Ben-Hadad promises to restore land

(20:34) and Ahab makes a treaty in which Ben-Hadad promises to restore the former Israelite territories. It was a treaty that would never be kept (see 22:3) and Ben-Hadad, king of Aram, would later give orders for Ahab to be killed (22:31). Ahab's generosity was misguided.

But more serious than misguided generosity, Ahab's 'mercy' was disobedience to the requirement of the Mosaic law that there should be no mercy given to Canaanite religion and no treaty ever made with those who promoted idolatry in the land of Israel. Ahab's 'mercy' to Ben-Hadad is in fact the worst kind of compromise with wickedness.

We tend at first to feel that Ahab has done something noble, but we must not be so hasty. Ben-Hadad's nation was pagan and wicked. God was inviting Ahab back to the Mosaic law, back to obedience to Him. God had given Ahab demonstrations of His power and had proved repeatedly the powerlessness of the pagan gods. Twice over (20:1–22, 23–34) He had proved the trustworthiness of His prophet.

What God had said about pagan religion was *'I will wipe them out'* (Exodus 23:23); *'I will hand over to you the people who live in the land . . . Do not make a covenant with them . . . Do not let them live . . . They will cause you to sin'* (Exodus 23:31–33). In the light of the Mosaic law that applied before the outpouring of the Spirit, the pathway of obedience for Ahab would have been the execution of Ben-Hadad II.

Once again a prophet is sent to Ahab. He is to present himself as an injured man, and so in the name of God he asks a fellow prophet to strike him savagely (20:35). What injuries and indignities prophets have to endure! No wonder they are famous for patience amidst sufferings (James 5:10). The fellow prophet refuses and suffers death himself because of his disobedience to the prophetic word (20:35–36). So serious a matter is a word that truly comes from God.

A second fellow prophet is more cooperative (20:37) and the man with a word for Ahab is injured. He goes as an injured man to speak to Ahab (20:38) and 'confesses' to the sin of letting a valuable prisoner escape (20:39–40a). The king knows how such carelessness should be punished (20:40b) and pronounces the death sentence upon the play-acting prophet (20:40b). Then the prophet removes his disguise and pronounces God's sentence upon Ahab himself. He will soon forfeit his life as a punishment for his 'mercy' upon paganism (20:41–42). Ahab responds with resentment but there is no sign of any willingness to turn to God for forgiveness and restoration (20:43).

What are the lessons of the story?

1. **The goodness of God invites Ahab to repentance**. Ahab sees demonstration after demonstration that God's word is addressing him. There is every reason for God to abandon Ahab altogether, but God is amazingly slow to leave Ahab to the folly of his own ways. It will happen eventually, but God is slow to judge and gives Ahab one opportunity after another to return to faith in the God of Abraham, Isaac and Jacob.

2. **What God is wanting is radical obedience**. Ahab is happy to get help from God. To some extent he is willing to follow prophetic guidance but he has no heart for radical obedience. In two major battles God has given very specific guidance to Ahab. But in as important a matter as the life or death of Ben-Hadad II he seeks no prophetic guidance. He had done so before (20:14) but fails here.

Many great failures in life come because we want a certain amount of guidance but not too much! One day, something comes before us and we act impulsively **without seeking God's guidance**. Ahab's impulsive act of mercy seemed so generous, but it was foolish. It was defying God's law. It was letting a vicious enemy free, an enemy whose army would soon kill Ahab (22:29–39) and whose successors would harrass Israel in days to come (2 Kings 10:32; 13:3). So great and vicious an evil was ancient paganism. If Ahab did not execute Ben-Hadad, Ben-Hadad would soon kill him. The spiritual principle remains. We must 'execute' the enemies of God in our life – sins and satanic temptations. Or else they will soon kill us!

Chapter 32

Naboth's Vineyard
(1 Kings 21:1–29)

God's law has many aspects to it. The next story deals with
the law concerning inherited land.

1. **We see God's concern to legally protect the individual**.
Naboth owned a vineyard that Ahab wanted (21:1–2), but it
was illegal for family inheritance to be sold permanently,
although it could be temporarily leased, so Naboth refused
(21:3).

The law prevented excessive wealth being accumulated by
powerful individuals, and it prevented the weak from being
totally landless. In some countries individuals use land only
by permission of the king. But in Israel each family could
claim that its possession of land was guaranteed by God
himself. Naboth's land was not his to sell. God's law
demanded that he keep it for the benefit of his family.

This gave security to the families of Israel. It enabled a
private citizen to withstand the pressure of a king! Ahab
was sullen and angry but did not feel he could get around
the law (21:4). Even in backslidden northern Israel the
prestige of the Mosaic law was sufficient to protect Naboth
and restrain the king.

Jezebel discovers Ahab sulking (21:5–6). Her ideas about
law and kingship are altogether different. *'Is this how you act
as king?'*, she asks (21:7). The Israelite king was meant to
write a copy of the Mosaic law (Deuteronomy 17:18) and
read it all of his life (Deuteronomy 17:19). The king was not

to *'consider himself better than his brother'*. Such obedience
to the law gave the king long life for himself and stability to
his dynasty (Deuteronomy 17:20). Jezebel wants none of
this. Her idea of kingship is that the king does whatever he
likes!

Yet even Jezebel cannot **ignore** the Mosaic law. In Ahab's
name she proclaims a fast (21:8). She then uses false
witnesses to accuse Naboth of cursing God and the king
(21:9–10a); this will lead to his execution (21:10b). Jezebel's
plan succeeds (21:11–14).

2. **We see then the weakness of the Mosaic law**. The law
protected the rights of the individual where it was obeyed,
but the presence of the law in Israel did not give Ahab a new
heart, and did not give him a love of righteousness. The law
dealt mainly with externals. It was administered before
judges. Someone could bring *'a charge against Naboth in the
presence of the people'* (21:13). The Christian is not 'under
the law' in this manner. The leading of the Spirit goes
deeper than anything we have here. The Spirit does not lead
by law-courts. He leads from within.

The law can be manipulated. Jezebel breaks the law,
introducing false witnesses (see Exodus 20:16, the ninth
commandment). And she commits murder (see Exodus
20:13, the sixth commandment). She is **using** the law to
break the law! It is the Mosaic law that demands two
witnesses (Deuteronomy 17:6), that forbids cursing God or
the king (Exodus 22:28) and that demands the death penalty
for such a crime (Leviticus 24:15–16). Jezebel is using the
law to evade the law. Naboth is being **legally** executed! The
Jewish leaders said concerning Jesus, *'We have a law and by
our law he ought to die'* (John 19:7). They used **law** to crucify
Jesus.

Again, all of this contrasts with the *'law of the Spirit'*. The
Holy Spirit cannot be manipulated. The Mosaic law was
administered by fallible law-courts. The Holy Spirit is
Witness and Convicter and Advocate all in one. He takes
the whole procedure for leading us in the pathway of righteousness upon himself and He makes no mistakes.

3. **Vindication, for Naboth, was to be found beyond the grave**. After Ahab has taken over Naboth's property (21:15–16), God steps in. Why did God not save Naboth's life? God is at liberty to rescue us or not as is best for His purpose. He does not **always** rescue. The three men of Daniel 3:17, 18 realised this. *'Our God is **able** to deliver ... but even if He does not ... '*. God sometimes has a greater purpose. God did not rescue His Son and delivered Him up to the powers of darkness – but God saved the world in so doing. For Jesus the 'rescue' was beyond the grave, in His resurrection from the dead. Naboth's 'rescue' would come in eternal glory as one who had laid down his life for God's kingdom and its righteousness.

4. **God gives final warnings**. God stepped in at the point when Ahab thought he was about to enjoy his vineyard. The prophets were not only sent to denounce idolatry; they were sent to denounce economic exploitation. Elijah was sent to announce a gruesome judgement (21:17–19). Ahab's life will soon end. God had already announced that it was forfeited because of the 'mercy' to Ben-Hadad (20:42, 43). Elijah now sums up the message of Ahab's life: self-abandonment to evil (21:20) leading to the end of his line (21:21), promotion of the idolatry of Jeroboam (21:22), added iniquity in his following the counsel of Jezebel (21:23). God announces the total destruction of the line of Ahab in the most violent manner (21:24). His self-abandonment to wickedness has been the worst in Israel's history (21:25) with idolatry as its root cause (21:26).

At this late stage in life Ahab seems to respond to God's Word. The various times the Word of God has come to Ahab have been sufficient to convince him that this harsh message of God is likely to be as true as all the others have proved true. Ahab is shaken and responds for the first time positively to Elijah's word (21:27). Was Ahab's repentance genuine? God liked it (21:28–29a)! So it must have had something good in it. The judgement was delayed by Ahab's partial repentance (21:29b).

Chapter 33

Weak King and Bold Prophet

(1 Kings 22:1–28)

Ahab had released Ben-Hadad II, hoping to get back some lost territory. Now in an attempt to get some of it he himself is about to be killed. None of this would have arisen if Ahab had not released Ben-Hadad.

For three years Ahab is given a time of peace (22:1). Then Jehoshaphat of Judah visits Ahab of Israel (22:2). Jehoshaphat is a 'good' king (22:43) in that he did not support idolatry, but he is also weak and compromising. Ahab is the most wicked king Israel has ever had, and yet Jehoshaphat decides to do some friendly visiting (22:2)!

Ahab jumps at the opportunity to use Jehoshaphat. He cares nothing about him (as 22:30 will make clear). He draws him into war against Ben-Hadad (22:3–4a). Jehoshaphat misguidedly expresses his sense of brotherhood with Ahab (22:4b). *'I am as you are . . . '*, he says (22:5). On both sides there is a great display of friendliness but Jehoshaphat ought to be saying 'Ahab, get rid of your idolatry, and I might help you!'. Jehoshaphat is **not** as Ahab is. Jehoshaphat worships God; Ahab worships Baal. There could be no greater difference!

It soon becomes obvious that Jehoshaphat is in a false position. His attempts at witnessing do no good. Jehoshaphat wants to get guidance from 'Yahweh', the God who redeemed Israel by the blood of a lamb (22:5). He is trying

145

to practise his faith in Yahweh but he is in partnership with an idolater who worships Baal!

'Oh, do you want a prophecy?' says Ahab. 'Well, I have four hundred prophets working for me!' They gather the north Israelite prophets (22:6a) who all approve of Ahab's projected invasion (22:6b). It was a good thing to support the king and it was a good guess that he might win. It was the best their 'prophesying' could do! Ahab had defeated Ben-Hadad before and he now had Jehoshaphat with him. *'Go! Because the Lord, the sovereign One'* – the word Yahweh is not used – *'will give victory'* (22:6b).

Jehoshaphat is not convinced. He tries to witness for the Lord (22:7, 8). *'Is there not a prophet from Yahweh . . . ?'* (22:7). He is still trying to stand for his faith in Yahweh, the true God. But he is in a 'federation-of-religions'; false prophets are in a majority and are unanimous in their message (22:9–12).

'Well', says Ahab, 'we do have a prophet in the country who talks about Yahweh, but it is no good trying to deal with him! Whenever one of my prophets speaks this fellow always disagrees. He is very uncooperative but if you really want someone who says he is speaking for Yahweh, the only one around is this fellow Micaiah. But I warn you, you won't get anything helpful from him. He'll start talking to you about sin and judgement and that sort of stuff!' (see 22:8a).

Jehoshaphat is still trying to witness. 'You should not say things like that about a prophet of Yahweh', he says (22:8b).

'I'll send for him', says Ahab (22:9). So the kings sit on thrones, wicked Baal-worshipper alongside worshipper of Yahweh, in this foolish partnership (22:10). A 'prophet' named Zedekiah is doing his best to put on a good performance for the king, with a dramatic representation, made for the occasion (22:11). Everyone is in agreement (22:12).

Someone takes Micaiah aside before he arrives. 'My friend', says his advisor, 'there are four hundred prophets out there and they all agree that Ahab is going to defeat Ben-Hadad. Don't spoil our unity by giving some message about Yahweh as the true God. Why don't you just say something that will fit the occasion? If you join in with us, maybe you will have opportunities to share the way you feel on future occasions' (22:13).

Micaiah replies. 'I am not trying to support comfortable state-religion. God gives me His word and I share it. It is as simple as that! I do not know any way I can pretend God has said something other than what He has said' (22:14)!

Micaiah goes into the presence of the kings and is asked the question, *'Should Ahab and Jehoshaphat attack Ben-Hadad?'* (22:15a).

'I can tell what you want me to say. If you want me to say it, I'll say it. The Lord will give you the victory! There! Now you have what you want!' (22:15b).

'Don't play games with us' says Ahab. 'Tell us properly what your message is' (22:16).

'Do you really want to know? I was given a vision of the northern kingdom. The nation was a flock of sheep without a shepherd. The battle was lost, the king was dead, and the people were running for home. Ahab, if you go into this battle you will die' (see 22:17).

'I told you this would happen', says Ahab. 'That's typical of the stuff you get from this fellow. I have four hundred prophets who help me but this man claims to prophesy in the name of Yahweh and he always comes out with these messages threatening judgement on me' (22:18).

'I can tell you more', says Micaiah. 'In my vision God allowed a lying spirit to deceive these four hundred prophets of yours' (22:19–23a). If you go into this battle, you will soon have finished with this world for ever (22:23b).

Micaiah's witness from outside is more powerful than Jehoshaphat's witness as a compromiser.

At this point the friendly atmosphere suffers a breakdown! One of the religious leaders decides that tolerance has gone too far in allowing Micaiah to speak. He'll tolerate anything in this religious set-up, Baal-worship, sacred prostitution, anything! But not someone claiming to have a word from God. He slaps Micaiah on the face (22:24), accuses Micaiah of himself having a lying spirit (22:25) and Micaiah is put in prison (22:26–27). So much for loving friendliness between Baal and Yahweh! Jehoshaphat's friendly visit to Ahab was turning out to be not so friendly after all. Jehoshaphat does nothing to help his fellow worshipper of Yahweh, Micaiah. He can sit on a throne next to Ahab but will not stand by his fellow believer in trouble. Micaiah goes into prison still insisting that his word is a word from God (22:28). He was soon vindicated (see 22:29–40). Everything he said came true. Four hundred prophets were proved to be false prophets. Jehoshaphat himself escaped death only because he cried to God for mercy (22:32–33). His attempts at compromise and friendliness with Ahab were discredited.

God's Word stands over against human guesswork. Faith in the God of Israel cannot be mixed with 'religions'. Better a suffering witness that stands for God's truth than a compromising 'friendliness' which will soon be exposed as worthless.

Chapter 34

A Stray Arrow

(1 Kings 22:29–40)

God's word will certainly be fulfilled. God watches over His word to bring it to pass.

1. **God likes to save us and bless us through sending us His word**. Time and time again Ahab had received revelations from God. On mount Carmel he had seen demonstrations of God willingness to honour His prophet Elijah and hear Elijah's prayers. He had seen God's control of the rain. Twice a prophet had given him guidance in battle against Ben-Hadad II. God has a habit of giving warnings and promises. On this occasion Ahab had been told that if he went into battle against Ramoth-Gilead he would lose his life.

It is a great privilege to have God speak to us. God may speak even to a wicked person. Ahab was a wicked man but God was concerned about northern Israel, and was still giving messages even to this wicked king of the north.

If Ahab had taken note of God and had pleaded to God for mercy the entire history of Israel might have been different.

2. **God likes His word to be received with faith**. God can give us promises and He can send us warnings. Either way He wants to be believed. He wants us by faith and patience to inherit the promises. Or He wants us by faith and amending of our life to turn aside His threats. Whatever kind of word it is that God gives, He wants us to respond with faith.

God dislikes double-mindedness. A double-minded man is unstable in all his ways and receives nothing from the Lord.

Ahab had a divided mind about God's Word. On the one hand he was refusing to believe the warning that had come to him through Micaiah the prophet. He had been told that if he went into battle against the king of Syria he would be killed. Yet he was refusing to believe the warning (22:29) and went into the battle disregarding the word he had received from one of God's prophets. And yet he had a secret fear that that word might be true after all because he was doing what he could to make sure it did not come to pass. He went into battle in disguise so that no enemy soldier could specially aim to kill him (22:30). He was *'supressing the truth'* (Romans 1:18). He was like the wicked man of Psalm 10:13 who says *'He will not call me to account'*. He was actually doing everything he could to prevent the Word of God being fulfilled. He persuaded Jehoshaphat to wear his royal robes. 'You be the leader of the battle', he said to the king. 'I'll just be an ordinary soldier'. Poor Jehoshaphat! He was still reckoning Ahab was a man to be friendly with, although Ahab was virtually sending Jehoshaphat to his death! But Ahab fears that the Word of God might come true after all. Micaiah was quite convincing!

3. **When God decides to fulfil His Word nothing can stop Him**. God's warnings may be turned aside by repentance. In this sense God's threat could be restrained. But Ahab is not doing any repenting, so the Word of God's warning is about to be fulfilled.

The Syrians are looking exclusively for Ahab, seeking to kill him (22:21). Everything seems against God's Word at this point. The king is in disguise. Another person is dressed as king and so is attracting the attention of the enemy. Jehoshaphat almost loses his life and is only saved through his plea to God and God's mercy (22:32–33). Ahab is wearing heavy armour. There seems to be no likelihood that Ahab is about to lose his life.

But God's word has been spoken; it is about to be fulfilled. *'Someone drew his bow at random and hit the king of*

Israel between the sections of his armour . . . ' (22:34a). What did the king think in those moments? He lived long enough to remember that God's word had been fulfilled (22:34b). All day long he pretended to be well (22:35) but that evening he died. Micaiah's prophecy was fulfilled. Soon the people were scattering like sheep without a shepherd (22:36, fulfilling 17). The prophecy of Elijah was also fulfilled (22:37-38, fulfilling 21:19). Ahab's achievements are listed (22:39) but his life is over (22:40). It contained nothing but wickedness. He had received message after message from God but now must give an account before God himself.

How strikingly the Word of God was fulfilled in Ahab's life. Every word to him proved true. It is easy for God to fulfil His Word. All circumstances of life are ruled by Him. All happenings in the world, great or small, are superintended by Him. *'The lot is cast into the lap but its every decision is from the LORD!'* (Proverbs 16:33). No enemy can frustrate His plans. He laughs at the pagan kings who think they can prevent His will from taking place. How feeble is Ahab's disguise. Even armour has chinks and gaps. God can guide a stray arrow to its precise destination in His will.

God's Word gets fulfilled. A princess can desire a baby and find herself looking after God's Saviour Moses. Saul can go insane and need the music of a shepherd boy to give him peace of mind – and so gives that very boy experience in the palace ready for his work as the next king. Eleven brothers can burn with jealousy and so send their twelfth brother ahead to Egypt to be ready to provide them with corn twenty years. *'You meant it for evil'*, Joseph would say, *'but God meant it for good'* (Genesis 50:20).

Someone makes a telephone call . . . someone writes a letter . . . someone is standing on a street corner as you happen to walk by . . . someone comes to the meeting and you happen to get talking . . . *'Someone drew his bow at random'* . . . and the promise of God comes to pass.

Chapter 35

The Zeal of the Lord

(1 Kings 22:41–53)

Ahab is a study in sin, but Jehoshaphat and Ahaziah are studies in traditionalism.

1. **Jehoshaphat is an example of a good person who simply 'keeps the machinery going'** (22:41–50). He was generally right with God (22:41–43a), but was not sufficiently aggressive to do anything about the 'high places' (22:43b). His greatest weakness was his compromise with northern Israel. He made peace with Ahab (22:44). He achieved a few things. He waged war against God's enemies (22:45) and opposed immorality (22:46). Apparently he had an easy relationship with Edom (22:47). One of his ventures in business failed (22:48) and so did the occasion when northern Israel again wanted to be in some kind of partnership with him. On that occasion he refused (22:49). He died and was given honourable burial (22:50). But the sum total of his life was that he kept the wheels of machinery turning but did not change the situation in Judah. When God calls us to inherit a ministry it is easy just to 'keep things going', but what is needed is a plan from God and major progress towards the fulfilling of His will. At this point Jehoshaphat failed.

2. **Ahaziah is an ungodly king who kept going the traditional sins of his culture (22:51–53).** Jehoshaphat 'kept the machinery turning over' in a nation that worshipped Yahweh, the God who saved Israel by atoning blood. Ahaziah was worse, a king who 'kept the machinery turning

over' not in the ways of righteousness but in the ways of wickedness. He continued in **traditional** sin. Sometimes certain sinful ways get entrenched in the life of a nation. Nations may have national sins. One thinks of some modern nations. Some have entrenched racisim or discrimination. Others have entrenched obsession with material wealth. Other are preoccupied with military strength. We are born into nations that have certain sinful ways. The question is will we continued in the vain traditions inherited from our fathers? Amaziah once again *'walked in the ways of his father and mother'*.

3. **A true son of David is to be a king neither in wickedness nor lukewarmness but in zeal**. It is not enough to 'keep the machinery going'. It brings no blessing to us to continue in traditonal godliness. I suppose it is better to be in traditonal godliness than in traditional ungodliness! But what God is looking for is zeal for Himself. He is looking for people who not only practise traditional godliness but also carry His kingdom forward.

Jehoshaphat is not Ahaziah. At least he was not entrenched in wickedness. And yet it cannot be said that he did a great deal for God either. You could never say of Jehoshaphat that *'the zeal of the Lord consumed him'*.

It was said of Jesus *'The zeal of the Lord consumed him'*. God was looking for a 'son of David', but of all of the kings we have seen thus far none of them can be said to be a true 'son of David'. David was a man after God's own heart. One only has to read the book of Psalms to see that what governed him was a passionate love of God. This book of Kings has so far considered fourteen kings, five of them direct successors to David. Solomon was foolish in tolerating the idolatries of his wives, and ended up tolerating pagan gods (1 Kings 11:33). Rehoboam was oppressive and, influenced by his Ammonite mother (14:21), introduced more of the detestable practises of the Canaanites (14:24). Abijah of Judah continued in ways of his father (15:3). Then for a generation we had hopes that a true son of David would be found. Asa of Judah did what was **right** (15:11) but he did not remove high places. Jehoshaphat of Judah was like Asa his father (22:43) but no descendant of David has had the zeal to remove the high places and the idolatry that is beginning to pervade Judah.

The nine kings in the north have been even worse. Jeroboam turned to idolatry (14:9). His son Nadab did no better, and his line came to an end. A second dynasty (Baasha, Elah) appeared and passed away, and a third dynasty appeared with Zimri but did not survive long. After a brief few days of Timni rule the dynasty of Omri commenced but Ahab his son and Ahaziah his grandson only intensified the evil of the northern kingdom.

Where is a true 'son of David' to be found? The earthly line of king David would never produce a true 'son of David', a man after God's own heart. Eventually the kingship would end altogether, a failed experiment. But the house of David would continue and out of the house of David would come a true son of David indeed. One day Jesus would be born in David's royal line, born in Bethlehem David's city. He would be anointed with the Spirit like David. The Spirit would come down on Him and rest upon him from that day forward (see 1 Samuel 16:16). God's 'son of David' would be characterised by zeal. In Him all the promises to the line of David begin to be fulfilled.

In Jehoshaphat we have mediocrity; in Ahaziah continued wickedness. Only when God's own 'son of David' would come would there be One in the line of David who would no longer be limping between two opinions (1 Kings 18:21) but aflame for God and His kingdom. Of Him it would be said the *'zeal of your house has eaten me up'* (Psalm 69:9; John 2:17). He would be the One who comes because the LORD *'saw that there was no one ... no one to interpose himself'*. *'His own arm brought salvation ... He wrapped Himself with zeal as with a mantle'* (Isaiah 59:16–17), and came in the person of His Son, our Lord Jesus Christ, Son of David.

Appendix

Some Facts About 1 and 2 Kings

Matters of 'Introduction' do not receive detailed discussion in this book. More detailed information of this nature can be found in D.J. Wiseman's *1 and 2 Kings* (Tyndale, 1993) and Howard F. Vos's *1, 2 Kings* (Zondervan, 1989).

E.R. Thiele's *Mysterious Numbers of the Hebrew Kings* (which deciphers the chronology of Kings) is in style half-way between a detective story and a telephone directory and very helpful. I have profited from Kevin J. Connor, *The Temple of Solomon* (Conner Publications, 1988) and enjoyed John Bunyan's *Solomon's Temple Spiritualised*. They have information not found in the twenty or so main commentaries which English-speaking preachers are likely to consult.

The books of 1 and 2 Kings are actually only one book in the Hebrew original. It was apparently first divided into two books by the Greek translators in the third century BC. The division at 1 Kings 22:53 is quite artificial and comes in the middle of Ahaziah's reign. Elijah's story is spread over the two books.

Five questions will lead us into what we need to know about 1 and 2 Kings.

Who wrote it? A historically minded prophet in the 6th century BC, whose name and identity is unknown, put it together using many sources that were available to him. It seems that the book of Deuteronomy kept on being enlarged with historical supplements which were written in the same style as the book of Deuteronomy, which itself comes mainly from the days of Moses. At one point there must have been Deuteronomy-Joshua. Then it got enlarged a bit more and there was Deuteronomy-Joshua-Judges, something like an expanded Deuteronomy, a third edition of Israel's history, all written in the same style. Then there was a 'fourth edition', Deuteronomy-Joshua-Judges-Samuel. Then finally there was Deuteronomy-to-2 Kings, all written in the 'Deuteronomic' style and all building upon the teaching of the book of Deuteronomy.

When was it written? It seems that 1, 2 Kings as we have it has to be dated in the middle sixth century. It is the last section of the full story in Deuteronomy-to-2 Kings, completed in the sixth century as a kind of 'fifth edition' of Israel's history. It has to be dated after the death of Jehoiachin because of the phrase 'as long as he lived' in 2 Kings 25:27–30, the latest event in the book.

Why was it written? The wise men and prophets of Israel felt it useful to keep a record of the things God had done within Israel's history. So, under the inspiration of the Holy Spirit they felt led to compile this history for the benefit of later ages. Its main purpose seems to have been to demonstrate from history the folly of idolatry.

How was it written? The author-editor of Kings used sources (see 1 Kings 11:41: 14:29 and similar references elsewhere). Some fragments of history had already been written and an author-editor put it all together. Some scholars think they can reconstruct what the sources were. They may be right, but it is hard to prove the scholars are doing anything more than guessing.

How does the story unfold? 'Kings' unfolds chronologically. Each king of Judah in the south is evaluated according to the way he forwards the promise given to David (2 Samuel 7:12–16). Northern kings are all condemned for continuing the sins of Jeroboam I, who made Israel to sin. With regard to 1 Kings the outline and chronology are as follows.

1 Kings 1:1–11:43 Israel's 3rd king, Solomon. His co-regency with David (chs. 1:1–2:46), his marriage, the building of the temple, and its dedication (3:1–9:9), God's covenant with and Solomon, the visit of the queen of Sheba (9:10–11:43).

1 Kings 12:1–24 The division of the kingdom.

1 Kings 12:25–14:20 4. Jeroboam I of Israel (930–909 BC)

1 Kings 14:21–14:31 5. Rehoboam of Judah (931–913 BC)

1 Kings 15:1–8 6. Abijam of Judah (913–910 BC)

1 Kings 15:9–24 7. Asa of Judah (910–870 BC)

1 Kings 15:25–32 8. Nadab of Israel (909–908 BC)

1 Kings 15:33–16:7 9. Baasha of Israel (908–866 BC)

1 Kings 16:8–14 10. Elah of Israel (886–885 BC)

1 Kings 16:15–21 11. Zimri of Israel (885 BC)

1 Kings 16:22–28 12. Tibni and 13. Omri (885–880; 885–874 BC)

1 Kings 16:29–22:40 14. Ahab of Israel (874–853 BC)

1 Kings 22:41–51 15. Jehoshaphat of Judah (873–848 BC)

1 Kings 22:51–53 16. Ahaziah of Israel (853–852 BC)

If you have enjoyed this book and would like to help us to send a copy of it and many other titles to needy pastors in the **Third World**, please write for further information or send your gift to:

Sovereign World Trust
PO Box 777, Tonbridge
Kent TN11 9XT
United Kingdom

or to the **'Sovereign World'** distributor in your country.

If sending money from outside the United Kingdom, please send an International Money Order or Foreign Bank Draft in STERLING, drawn on a **UK** bank to **Sovereign World Trust**.